Middle School: The Stuff Nobody Tells You About

A Teenage Girl with High-Functioning Autism Shares Her Experiences

Haley Moss

Preface by Susan J. Moreno
Foreword by Diane Adreon

PUBLISHING

P.O. Box 23173
Shawnee Mission, Kansas 66283-0173
www.aapcpublishing.net

© 2010 AAPC Publishing
P.O. Box 23173
Shawnee Mission, Kansas 66283-0173
www.aapcpublishing.net

Publisher's Cataloging-in-Publication

Moss, Haley.

    Middle school: the stuff nobody tells you about : a teenage girl with high-functioning autism shares her experiences / Haley Moss. -- 1st ed. -- Shawnee Mission, Kan. : Autism Asperger Pub. Co., c2010.

        p. ; cm.
        ISBN: 978-1-934575-62-8
        LCCN: 2010921017

        1. Middle school students--United States--Life skills guides. 2. Teenage girls--Education (Middle school)--United States--Handbooks, manuals, etc. 3. Middle schools--Social aspects--United States. 4. Asperger's syndrome in adolescence--Patients--Education (Middle school)--United States--Handbooks, manuals, etc. 5. Autistic youth--Education (Middle school)--United States--Handbooks, manuals, etc. 6. Social skills in adolescence. 7. Adolescent psychology. I. Title.

LB1623.5 .M67 2010   2010921017
373.236/0973--dc22   1002

This book is designed in Helvetica Rounded and Helvetica Neue. Cover and interior illustrations: Haley Moss. Printed in the United States of America.

Acknowledgments

I'd like to thank my parents, Sherry and Rick, for everything that they have done for me since day one. We expected a long journey together through autism, from the day of diagnosis all the way until now and beyond. Your love and support cannot be matched by anyone else's in my life, and there is no way in the world I could thank you properly for all that you have done for me throughout my life. I love you guys the most!

I want to thank my uncle Scott for flying into Florida on every special occasion of mine, whether my fifth-grade graduation or my first art show. I love you Scotty Doodle! Grandparents and great-aunts, I love you, too. Thanks for always sticking by me and encouraging me.

I'd also like to thank the AAPC family, especially my wonderful editor, Kirsten McBride, Keith and Brenda Myles, and Carly Halvorson. They have been my partners throughout the book-writing process, and this book would not be in your, the reader's, hands without the time and effort they have put into this book.

I'd also like to thank my enormous family at the University of Miami C.A.R.D. (Center for Autism and Related Disabilities) for giving my family hope, direction and advice through this journey through autism. I especially want to thank Diane Adreon and Natalee George for providing me many opportunities to give back to such a great organization so that others on the autism spectrum can receive the help and guidance they need.

There is another special person that I have met in the "autism world" who has been my cheerleader and champion since the day we met. I love you, Susan Moreno! I look forward to continuing to work with you and MAAP!

Many thanks to all of my teachers at the Day School at Coral Springs. I also want to thank the administration and all of my teachers from Pine Crest School in Fort Lauderdale for giving me the willpower to push forward and continue to grow as a person. They have inspired me and given me the confidence to express myself both artistically and literally. Thank you PC! Go Panthers forever!

There are specific people at both of these schools who have helped me along the way whom I want to thank. At the Day School, Mrs. Deborah Williams, Ms. Emily Frey, Mr. John Kranstover, Mr. Mark Heller, Mrs. Adena Shriner and Ms. Janet Diamond. At Pine Crest, Dr. Lourdes Cowgill, Mrs. Ani McKee, Ms. Estes Carns, Dr. Dana Markham, Mr. Jeff Rothstein, Mr. James Patrick, Ms. Elizabeth Hanlon, Mrs. Barbara Smith, Ms. Marla Tapper, Ms. Toni Marshall and staff and Mr. Stu Opperman.

Acknowledgments

I also want to mention another important and special person who has influenced and changed my life for the best! Gallery owner Joe Aronstein "discovered" my art and gave me the once-in-a-lifetime opportunity to have wall space in his gallery to show and sell my work to the public and to help me share my story to help raise money for autism.

I want to thank the entire Hertz Parkland Jewelers family for their continuous support of me and the autism community. They have teamed up with me to raise money for autism while raising awareness. I especially want to thank Scott Hertz, Jo-Ann Van Der Merwe, Eitne Van Der Merwe and Dawn Ehlin.

The "friendship front" isn't good for me at all times because of constantly changing friends. However, my adopted family, Aunt Vicky, Uncle Duke and "Cousin" Sydney, has always been there for me like friends and family, all wrapped up into one big package! You guys are the best and have been there the whole time!

Within the pages of the book, thanks to Kristi and Kaede Sakai, Jamie and Jen Blackwell as well as Melissa Trautman, who added their perspectives and comments to my story.

Finally, thanks to all the readers who are reading this right now. I hope this book helps you and you learn something new from what I have to share. We're all in this together! Our challenges become our strengths!

Haley

Preface

I first met Haley Moss three years ago. It was a life-changing experience. Haley was speaking on a panel about her thoughts and experiences as a young woman with high-functioning autism. That is a pretty big assignment for any first-time speaker – add to that being only thirteen years old.

Haley exhibited both poise and wisdom – made even more remarkable by her young age. She was on a panel of very talented and articulate individuals on the autism spectrum. Yet, still she shone like a star. Her lovely speaking voice and her beauty were great enhancements to her success. In addition to her upbeat attitude and enthusiasm for life and the future, what struck me most deeply was Haley's response to the question, "How did your parents tell you that you were on the autism spectrum?" She had asked her mom why she was different from her classmates and her mom had replied, "You have magical powers!" Haley had explained that she was very into Harry Potter, so her mom had followed the gist of those wonderful books in explaining her differences. That moment, Haley and her mom, Sheri, touched my heart and my soul. Norman Vincent Peale could take lessons from the Moss family in positive attitude and energy.

As I stayed in touch with the Moss family through emails and phone calls, I began to think of Haley as "the little comet." She is a bright and shining force soaring through life, who is just as rare and remarkable as the comet that shares her name, although with a slightly different spelling.

It was only after meeting the Moss family and spending time with them that I learned of Haley's incredible artistic talent. When Haley told me she had written her first book, I worried that someone with that much talent in art couldn't possibly have much talent left for writing. But my worries were unfounded.

In the process of growth from infancy to adulthood, no time is more challenging than the middle school/junior high years. Bodies are changing, hormones are raging, and the often easy and gentle camaraderie and acceptance of the elementary school years evaporate with lightning speed, even for the most socially gifted students. Gossip, betrayal, bullying and general cruelty hit a fever pitch. Navigating the often frightening and sometimes heartbreaking journey through the middle school years can loom as an impossible task to students with an autism spectrum challenge and their parents.

Haley's advice and honest sharing of her successes and bumps in the road makes for helpful advice for students in or approaching middle school, but also lends a new perspective to parents, teachers and siblings.

It is time for you to begin your journey through junior

Preface

high/middle school with Haley. You are in for some excellent learning opportunities. Haley is quite thorough in her discussion of pitfalls that can often be avoided. An excellent example is her discussion of the middle school locker: varieties, etiquette and staging – an entire eight pages of it. While some writers could make eight pages on lockers into a tedious detour, Haley makes it worth your while, pointing out facets of the locker scene that many have never before considered. Her discussion also includes middle school slang, etiquette with teachers, ways to survive lunch, learning to adapt to the varying personalities and styles of teachers, safely gaining social acceptance and a host of other vital topics – often viewed from a new and practical perspective that is enhanced by Haley's artwork, which pops up throughout the book. Her art is delightful – I especially love her stressed-out-girl drawing.

I truly believe this book will help many middle school and pre-middle school girls. Their family members, friends, and teachers will also gain a new and helpful perspective on one of life's more challenging adventures: a successful middle school experience.

Fellow readers, fasten your seatbelts and get ready for the journey. Haley's comet is about to take off. I know you will enjoy the ride!

Susan J. Moreno, President
OASIS@MAAP
MAAP Services for Autism and Asperger Syndrome
www.aspergersyndrome.org

Foreword

I highly doubt that you have ever heard someone say,
"I wish I was back in middle school. Those were the days!"

For most students, middle school is a tough time. For students with autism spectrum disorders (ASD), it can be particularly difficult. In addition to academics, social demands also become more complex in adolescence, and there is great pressure to "fit in." In such a setting, children who are "different" are not well tolerated.

Haley Moss devoted a lot of time and energy during her early teen years to learning the "hidden curriculum" for middle school survival and social survival as a teenage girl. Her book spells out in great detail the hidden curriculum that students with ASD need to know – everything from school lockers, lunch, how to talk to teachers, to homework, time management and friendship. She also addresses hidden curriculum items specifically for girls.

This book also tells Haley's personal story of life in middle school. Haley's story is just that … Haley's story. In addition, the experiences and advice from other girls on the spectrum as well as a teacher's perspective are included. These sections enhance the richness of this wonderful guide to middle school.

Adults may find some sections particularly helpful. For example, the section on New Slang defines slang words and clarifies what kids are really saying. Haley also provides definitions of common Internet lingo.

I have had the pleasure of knowing Haley and her parents, Sherry and Rick, since Haley was a toddler. With her parents' loving help and guidance, Haley has progressed beautifully. She made a decision fairly recently to "come out" and tell people about her autism. She decided that she wanted to do something that would help people with ASD. This book will help many adolescents with ASD and their families.

You can only imagine my delight at seeing how far Haley has come. She is a beautiful and lovely young lady. She is a high achiever in school and a talented writer. And, as you can see from her artwork throughout the book, she is a talented artist as well. Understandably, her parents are very proud of her accomplishments. Personally, I am proud of her, and I believe that the autism community takes pride in learning about and from people with ASD like Haley.

– Diane Adreon is the associate director of the University of Miami-Nova Southeastern University Center for Autism & Related Disabilities (UM-NSU CARD). She has written several articles on high-functioning autism and Asperger Syndrome and has co-authored two books: *Simple Strategies That Work! Helpful Hints for all Educators of Students with High-Functioning Autism, Asperger Syndrome, and Related Disabilities* (with Myles & Gitlitz), and *Asperger Syndrome and Adolescence: Practical Solutions for School Success* (with Myles). The latter is the winner of the Autism Society of America's 2002 Outstanding Literary Work.

Table of Contents

Introduction

What's All the Fuss?

Hey girls and parents!

Middle school and junior high can be a very hard time. There are new friends to be made, new schedules, new teachers, new buildings – pretty much everything is new. Middle or junior high school typically consists of sixth, seventh and eighth grade. This may be different depending on what district you live in.

Middle or junior high school is nothing like elementary school. You are not with the same twenty to thirty kids every single class, as you are not all taking the exact same classes. Academic demands are heavier. Snack time and recess are things of the past. You will have more responsibilities, such as being organized, managing your time and deciding what sports teams and extracurricular activities to join.

In this book, I will discuss what you can expect in middle school and how to prepare yourself. I will share issues like the size of a classroom or the bell ringing, how to deal with slightly more "mature" peers, how to handle teachers and, of course, the real reason why you are even enduring middle school: the academics. In other words, we will look at what you've got to do so you can move ahead in life.

Since my issues and challenges may be a bit different from yours, I have asked other middle school kids

Introduction

to add their thoughts in certain places, as a way to give you even more ideas. And finally, a teacher adds her thoughts and advice throughout – again, in an effort to give you as much support as possible.

I'd like to start off this middle school "survival guide" with a few words about myself. My name is Haley. I'm fourteen years old, and I have high-functioning autism. I am described as quiet, stubborn, beautiful, kind – and someone who can explain herself. I am very honest. I'm not going to tell you "middle school was great!" and only share the good things. I will share all the important middle school experiences I've had – the good, the bad and the ugly.

So far, I believe it was the hardest time of my life. I went to three different schools in three years. All were different in every way – they offered different opportunities, different teaching styles, different-sized campuses and different student bodies. I've been through many odd situations such as girls accusing me of things I didn't do (one girl cyber-bullied one of my good friends and I was wrongfully given the blame), lunchroom horrors and on some evenings having so much homework I didn't go to bed until midnight.

Now that I am a freshman in high school, reflecting back on middle school triggers many memories, both good and bad. I would like to share my experiences and give you some advice so that your middle school years may be easier for you. I spearheaded the expedition so to speak: I hope you can learn from my mistakes, admire my successes and try to do the right things and make good choices for yourself.

I wish you lots of luck with your middle school or junior high adventures!

Haley

The Summer Break – Getting Ready

It is the night before the first day of school. After eating dinner with my family, I get my backpack ready and lay out the clothes I am going to wear tomorrow. I also shower so I won't feel so rushed in the morning, especially on the first day when everything will be new and unfamiliar. Because I am nervous, I want to get a good night's sleep, so I go to bed at 9:00. Besides, after the summer break when my schedule, including bedtime, was pretty loose, I have to get used to getting up early.

Summer has come to an end. Today is the "big day" – the first day of middle school.

I wake up at 6:30 a.m. and feel kind of nervous. I eat a big breakfast because my lunch is later in the day and I don't want to be hungry when I should be paying attention. After breakfast I brush my teeth, and I might even chew gum to make sure my breath smells okay. (If you have braces, gum is a no-no – eat a mint instead.) Then I put on deodorant and get dressed – I have chosen some of my new school clothes. I also put on my lucky necklace. Then I look at myself in the mirror, I think I look nice but decide to put on a little bit of lip gloss.

Most students in middle school take the bus, but my dad drives me every morning. This is lucky, as it means I don't have to leave as early as if I was taking the bus.

Since it is the first day at my new school, I get there a little early. First, I look for my locker, so I can put things away, such as pens and pencils. I smile at anyone who passes me, and I say hi to people who look like they are in my grade. I am shy, but saying hello isn't much of a stretch for me. I could wave if I am busy, or nod my head to let people know I see them.

Once I have locked my locker, the bell rings. It is loud and un-ignorable. I head to my first class. I check my watch to make sure I am on time. I don't want my teacher to think I am skipping class on the first day or that I am not being respectful by being late. Teachers seem to jump all over this respect thing. I am not a troublemaker, and I do not want to get in trouble.

My first-period class is world history. I sit next to a girl who has the locker below mine. I met her at orientation last week, and she was nice to me. Our teacher is very nice. He says he doesn't believe in tests, because he feels it doesn't help kids learn. He also says he will give homework no more than three days a week. He already knows all of us by name – talk about doing his homework. I feel relieved because he is a nice guy and tries not to create stress. No tests, little homework! This is awesome! He began by talking about Africa and the various cultural groups in this vast continent.

Next I have math. There are a lot of kids in this class. Our teacher gives us assigned seats, and I get to

Introduction

sit next to two boys who complain about how they are bad at math and that we will get too much homework.

The class begins with a review of math we did in elementary school. One of the kids asks the teacher how much money he makes. The teacher gets this twisted look on his face and then answers, "not enough." I tried to avoid that kid for the rest of the day. It is never good to ask teachers personal questions. If you wouldn't ask your friend's parents something, then you shouldn't even think about asking a teacher. Generally, the only good questions to ask teachers are those relating to what they teach.

In English, the girl I sat with in world history sits next to me again. I'm happy she is in my class! The teacher tells us to take out the book we were supposed to read over the summer. I actually read the book twice to make sure I understood it. She also assigns a project that is due in two weeks. She holds up a finished version of the project and explains how it should look. This is great, because I like being able to see things instead of hearing things, like many people who have ASD.

So far my day is going great – a new friend sits next to me in two classes and my first three teachers seem nice and organized.

However, science – the next class – turns out to be a bad experience. My teacher is very loud, she never smiles, and everything in that classroom is auditory-based. She never writes anything on the board, has no science posters in the room and provides nothing for me to look at to help make me understand. This won't work for me. When I get home tonight I will ask my mom to help me figure out what to do.

Next comes the biggest fear of the day: lunch. I'm happy to say that the girl from my world history and English classes once again came to my rescue. I did not know where to sit, but she came up to me and said, "Let's sit together; maybe we can meet some cute boys."

She wants me to meet boys with her! This is new to me. I have never had a crush on a boy. She is a very pretty girl who has self-confidence – and she chooses me to be her friend. I'm scared but excited. I don't know if I can pull this social stuff off. I tend to be shy and a loner, and she is very outgoing and self-confident. We sit with a group of football players that she is interested in.

The lunchroom is really loud, but I am able to hear everything World History Girl says to me. I have a friend for the beginning of school, even if we don't necessarily have much in common! It is nice to have someone to sit with on my first day. It makes school a lot easier.

I have to get used to lunch. The noise levels are off the chart – if it were just a little bit louder, the windows might have shattered. Secretly, I want to sit alone outside, but we have to stay in the lunchroom until we are dismissed. Besides, I know that I have to give being social a chance.

Gym is my least favorite thing of the day – next to science. My coach is mean and tough. She only likes athletes. She doesn't like me, because I don't know how to play volleyball. (I still don't to this day!) I try to change into my gym clothes quickly, so I won't upset my coach. She upset me by having me serve a volleyball when I had no idea what to do. The bell can't ring soon enough. Volleyball can wait until tomorrow.

Next is Spanish. My teacher is very nice and likes me, because I understand everything she says. I can recite the alphabet and spell my name in Spanish. Everyone in my class is older than me, because I am taking advanced Spanish. Most of them don't seem nice to me, probably because they can tell I am better at Spanish than they and our teacher likes me.

After Spanish I have an advisory period where I meet my advisor. She knows of my diagnosis. Everybody in my advisory group introduces themselves to each other. One girl comes up to me, says she likes my necklace and adds that she wants me to eat lunch with her tomorrow. I say yes and promise to meet her outside the cafeteria. ☺

My day is almost over. I am excited because I have only one more class – and I made two new friends!

Finally, I have art. Art is my favorite class of the day because it is relaxing. Art is something I think I am good *at. I sit next to a girl I remember from orientation. She is also good at art. That makes me feel even better.*

My day was long and I am exhausted. When my mom picks me up, she asks how it went. I tell her that I met some new friends. When we get home, I will tell her about the problem with my science class. I also tell her I have a feeling this year will be good.

> *I ended up switching to a different science class with a teacher who relied almost solely on visuals. We had to draw pictures in our notes of what we saw during labs, and she also had live animals and displays in her room. She was quiet and repeated herself often because the kids were a bit slower at picking things up than in my other class. I ended up winning the school science award that year.*
>
> *If you feel uncomfortable in a certain class, tell your parents early on (before the first two weeks of school are over, or the first test happens), so you can switch out of the class or make other accommodations.*

But let's backtrack and see what led up to this "big day."

Before we even get into anything, I want to emphasize that everybody (both boys and girls) is nervous about starting something new. It is perfectly normal to be afraid of the unknown. I am writing this "survival guide" so that by the time you enter middle school, it won't be so mysterious and you will have a heads-up, meaning that I told you a lot about what to expect so you won't be surprised. You will be ahead of everyone else. So relax and try to enjoy the rest of your summer.

Good Habits Before School Starts

Usually during the summer, people go to bed later than during the school year and sleep in. About two weeks before the first day of school, start gradually going to bed earlier and waking up earlier. During the summer I would go to bed around midnight. Two weeks before the start of school, I'd go to bed at 10:00 or 10:30 and get up at 8; halfway through that week I would go to bed at 10:00 and wake up at 7:30, and the next week I'd get up at 7:00. Ultimately, I'd wake up at 6:00 and go to sleep by 9:30 like on a normal school night. It's the easiest way to get ready so you're not super tired on the first day.

Also before school starts, it's a good idea to make a tentative schedule for how your routine before and after school works. Mine is like this:

MORNINGS
6:00 – Wake up and eat breakfast
6:15 – Brush my teeth, put on deodorant, get
       dressed, make sure backpack is ready (it's
       packed the night before)

6:30 – Brush my hair, put on perfume/makeup/shoes, anything else needed

6:50 – Put backpack in the car and make sure everything is perfect one last time, including my cell phone in case of emergency

6:55 -7:00 – Leave the house

7:30-7:45 – Arrive at school. Put anything in locker if needed

8:00 – First bell rings

… the rest of the day follows the school schedule

AFTERNOONS/EVENINGS

4:15-4:30 – Get home from school

4:30-4:45 – Download and listen to music, play with my dog, do something to relax after a long school day

4:45-6:00 – Work on homework

6:00 – Eat dinner with my parents

6:30 – Shower for the next day. If necessary, blow-dry hair for the morning as well. Showering at night saves time in the morning

7:00 – Finish homework

8:00-8:30 – If necessary, study for any upcoming tests

8:30 – Start getting ready for bed and the next day. Put all completed homework and textbooks in backpack. Brush teeth and undo bed

8:45 – Relax, playing video games, listening to music, hanging out, etc.

9:00-9:30 – Go to bed

Orientation

If you are reading this during the summer months before you start middle school in August or September, you most likely attended an orientation (perhaps several) to middle school in the spring. This is when you and your fellow students visit the campus, get your schedule, go from class to class, see where your locker is, get a feel for everything and meet your teachers face-to-face.

If your school doesn't have a formal orientation day, maybe you can create your own by visiting the school, talking to teachers, seeing where your locker is and practicing opening it, and getting your schedule early and walking through it with your parents. In most school districts, teachers and administrators report to school a week before the students do. It's a good idea to set up a visit to the school during this time so that you can get a feel for the campus, discuss your individual needs and, if you're lucky, meet a few of your teachers.

If you're a visual learner, ask for a map or make up your own. It will help the first couple of days, but after the beginning, you will know where everything is. If it helps you, take pictures of the school or check the district or school website for information.

Supplies

One of the easier things to do in preparation for the upcoming school year is to go school supply shopping. Get yourself a rolling backpack if the school is large, or a backpack you can easily hoist up and carry on your shoulders. Messenger bags are good options, too. Most of my friends had rolling or carry-on bags.

When it comes to backpacks, I always found hidden zipper compartments helpful, because I like to keep spare change in case I need a pay phone, an emergency pad in the girl's bathroom, or a snack. NOTE: Only bring small bills. Do not take all of your allowance money as it could get stolen. Try to take maybe $10 max and restock when needed. Keep up with this because you never know when you may have to buy something at school.

Your school may provide school supply lists. If it does, it's easy – you just go down the list and get everything you need. If your school doesn't give you a supply list, the teachers will tell you what they want you to buy. But it is always good to be prepared. So at the very least, bring paper and pencil so you can write down what you will have to get.

Like in elementary school, it's okay to have designer pencils, pink folders and notebooks with little flowers and similar designs on them. Not only is it okay, it makes it easier to recognize and always know your stuff from everyone else's. When you buy notebooks, it is a good idea to get a different color for each subject and label them accordingly. I had a green binder with a matching green notebook for math, pink folders and a pink notebook were for English, yellow for Spanish, etc. Some of my friends label their materials with adhesive-backed letters. These kinds of markings also make things easier to pull out of your backpack when you get to class and help you stay organized.

If your school requires uniforms, you and your mother or other adult should probably take care of that in the beginning of the summer (like June), because uniform stores get crowded and may run out of stuff.

If your school does not have a uniform, you may want to look at teenage fashion magazines such as *Seventeen* and *Cosmo Girl*, or pop stars like Miley Cyrus, to see what the kids are wearing. Most teen magazines have a back-to-school section of all the cool things to wear to school. You can also look at the store flyers in the Sunday papers to get ideas of what is popular before school starts.

Looking fashionable on the first day helps you make friends really quickly because girls will say how great you look. A good place to find cool accessories is Forever 21. Most accessories are under $10, and they always have all the current stuff that teenagers wear. If there isn't a Forever 21 in your area, Target, Wal-Mart and Claire's carry accessories that are reasonably priced.

As I mentioned, I've been to three different middle schools in three years. In sixth grade, I went to a small private school that I had already attended for five years. The middle school was located upstairs and was set apart from the elementary school. It was pretty much a continuation of elementary school – the same eighteen kids that I had known for the last five years were in all my classes. I wasn't challenged academically or socially.

The transition to middle school in sixth grade for me was not really a transition at all. The school administrators and teachers had known about my diagnosis for years and would work with me and my family. I had a great time in sixth grade. I was elected to the National Junior Honor Society and my grades were top notch. I won first place at the state science fair. Everything was going great for me, but I was bored.

Things changed drastically when, at the end of sixth grade, I asked my parents if I could attend a larger, technology-oriented private school. Computers were my thing; however, I knew the change would be challenging and exciting for me, both academically and socially. So, in seventh grade, I went to a school with a large campus.

Here I found out where everything was by following the other kids and exploring on orientation day. As usual, my parents spoke to the administration and my

Introduction

advisor about my diagnosis and asked them to keep a special eye on me in case there were any problems. I did not need any academic accommodations (I was in all honors classes).

I visited the school a few weeks before classes started to get used to the campus and meet other kids. The day before school, I went to orientation, got my books and school supplies and decorated my locker. I even met some new kids that day! I was excited to begin a new school year.

Unfortunately, my initial excitement didn't last long. I was not happy at the new school. I felt like I wasn't learning anything and was so bored that I was almost falling asleep in every class. The students had poor manners and showed no respect for their teachers or peers. Kids sometimes ignored what the teachers said or walked away when teachers were talking to them. Some kids yelled at each other and called each other names. It was even common to see physical fights.

Luckily, I wasn't bullied, but I just didn't fit in. I felt like I was alone. Neither my parents nor my teachers thought I belonged at that school, so change was necessary once more. It's surprising, but the large size of the campus didn't bother me.

Although I didn't learn much academically in seventh grade, I did learn a lot socially. My seventh-grade year was my social education year. I learned how to enter "girl world." I learned some of the secrets to fitting in (more on all this later). I did so well in seventh grade that I even got to participate in inducting new members to the National Junior Honor Society. I had my art displayed at the mayor's office and took third prize in my school's art show. I also won an award from Duke University for my score on a college entrance exam that I took for fun.

In eighth grade, I attended a school where the middle school was housed in one building and the eighth grade was held in one big room (which I called a "pod"). It had five classrooms inside of it, so it was easy to find everything. All of my teachers were friendly and ready to help, and the kids were generally polite and smart. Fitting in didn't seem like it would be that hard. Another plus of the school was that the lunchroom and gym weren't far from the "pod," so the layout reminded me of my sixth-grade and elementary school experience. I felt more relaxed and at home right away.

I had finally found the perfect school for me. I continue to attend this school, and I plan on graduating from high school there.

Even if you hate shopping, don't care for trends, don't like how charm bracelets clunk against your desk, etc., I suggest finding a fad that you think is doable. Ugg boots, or similar knock-offs, is one fad that many people with ASD love because they feel good on your feet. Funky socks, scarves and hats (don't wear inside the school building) are other ideas.

Introduction

Unfortunately, at this age and stage of your life, you are often judged by what you wear. I didn't make this up or write the rules. It's just how it is. Watch *Mean Girls* and you'll know exactly what I'm talking about. If it were up to me, it wouldn't be this way. I'd wear sweatpants, a t-shirt and no makeup every single day. But comfort isn't always the best option during the school day, or for making and keeping friends. It's a good idea to put some extra time and effort into how we look. The outside world cares. You should always look neat and clean no matter what.

A Teacher's Perspective

I agree with Haley that before school starts, it is important to visit the school that you will be attending and walk through your schedule. You can find your locker, get your locker combination and put supplies away. This will help reduce some of your anxiety around getting to class on time the first day of school. It's also a good idea to meet one of your teachers or a counselor in the building before school starts in case you have any questions or concerns on the first day. It's normal to be anxious and excited the first day of school. If you can prepare ahead of time, you'll be more comfortable and less anxious.

Chapter 1

New Places and New Faces – Challenges in Middle School

o matter what middle or junior high school you go to, whether it is private or public, chances are that the school will have three grades (sixth, seventh and eighth) all in the same building. Expect to have a schedule (with the time and place) of your core classes such as math, science, social studies, a foreign language and English, as well as maybe a course or two you choose yourself (see "Electives" in Chapter 4). You will be assigned a locker (more on lockers on page 24) and either a homeroom teacher or an advisor.

The homeroom teacher is usually the first teacher you have every day. He or she typically takes attendance and reads the school announcements before class begins. An advisor, on the other hand, is a teacher who helps you with any problems that arise at school. This could be social or academic. The advisor is supposed to be your go-to person at school. If you do not feel comfortable with your advisor, seek out help from your guidance counselor.

Some middle schools do not have homerooms or advisors. If that is the case in your school, try to find a staff member (teacher, counselor, secretary, etc.) that you can trust and go to if you have questions.

One thing is almost for certain: On the first day or two, almost everybody gets lost, so don't be afraid to ask an older student or a teacher where a certain classroom is. Besides, you will probably receive a map of your school or campus. On the first few days of school, it might be okay to be a few minutes late. However, do not make a habit of this because you will get in trouble. Try to learn your schedule and classroom locations as fast as you can.

Also during the first few days of school, you will be asked to dress up for Picture Day. On Picture Day, photographers come to take a picture of every student in the school. The pictures are used for school ID cards and the yearbook, so try and look your best. You need patience on that day. The lines are long, and you have to listen to the photographer's instructions: no funny faces or waving your arms. If you try to look natural, you will usually take a good picture. If you have trouble waiting in line, bring something to do, such as a book, an iPod, etc.

Middle school may pose sounds, sights and other things that are bothersome to you. There's your locker; that loud, annoying bell ringing approximately every 45 minutes; the constant chattering of people in the lunchroom and hallways; kids pushing and bumping into you in the hallways (usually by accident); hugs from friends; the bad smell of the locker rooms; the different food smells in the cafeteria; and the buzzing fluorescent lights of the classroom. Add to that the problems of where to sit at lunch and all the popular kids snickering about some new boy who is really skinny. Everything is new to you. None of this looks like elementary school.

Let's investigate how to tackle some of the hardest issues for people on the autism spectrum during middle school.

Lockers

Lockers are a little bit like "cubbies" in elementary school, except they're taller, thinner and have "doors" with locks on them. You have a locker because you can't carry everything you need throughout the day. Your books are typically heavy, and then there are notebooks, binders, pencils, etc., so it is easier to keep some of the things you don't need with you all the time in a locker.

You don't have to go to your locker all the time (most students visit their locker about three times a day: before school, before or after lunch, and at the end of the day). For example, get what you need for your morning classes in the morning, drop your morning stuff off in your locker before or after lunch and at the same time get the stuff you need for afternoon classes. Then after your afternoon classes, go back to your locker and get whatever books you need to study or do homework with and leave the rest. You may want to velcro a list inside the locker and inside your notebook that reminds you of when to go to your locker and what books to take with you each time.

The main issue with lockers is to know how to open the lock (see diagram next page). Combination locks have numbers ranging from 0-39. Three numbers in a specific order could make a combination.

For instance, let's say your locker combination is 22-12-26. Before you start, spin the little handle to "clear" the numbers from a previous opening of the lock. The first picture of the lock shows the arrow going clockwise (just like a clock, the "hands" move to the right). Try to be slow and accurate as you get to the first number. Slowly turn the handle until you reach 22. Once you reach 22, move the handle counterclockwise (to the left, see second picture in diagram). You will then pass 22, and stop on 12 – the second number in your combination. After you reach 12, move the handle clockwise to the last and final number (which in our case is 26), without passing the next number (you just do that on the counterclockwise movement). After you reach the final number, pull down and the lock opens.

If you have trouble with your lock, bring it home to practice opening it. Lock it around a shoelace or just in itself for additional practice. (If the lock is permanently attached to the locker in your school, perhaps you could purchase a combination lock to practice on at home.) If you don't think you will remember your combination, write it down somewhere safe such as in your wallet, or store it in your cell phone so you will be able to quickly access it. It is a good idea not to tell anyone your combination. Stealing goes on in schools more often than you may think. Basically, someone else knowing those three numbers is an invitation for your stuff to get stolen.

If you have a locker mate, don't keep anything valuable in your locker (iPod, phone, etc.). If you have to share lockers and you have a choice in the matter, try to pick a locker mate you already know and can trust.

If other kids are doing it, it's a good idea to decorate your locker. If you have the space, maybe add a shelf to organize your stuff (example: textbooks on top, notebooks on bottom). It might be cool to put stickers in the locker, a mirror on the side, and if there is room, a small poster of your favorite actor or musical artist in the back.

Some schools are strict about what is allowed as locker decorations, so check it out with your teacher. To play it safe, you may just want to add mirrors, shelves and things you can easily remove at the end of the year. If you do decide to decorate your locker, practice on a piece of paper first. For instance, if you want little flower stickers in your locker, try putting one on a piece of paper first. If you can't get it off, it's an indication that you shouldn't put it on your locker as it will adhere too firmly and you will have trouble removing it when the school year is over and you have to clean out your locker. One thing you could do to play it safe is to put the piece of paper covered in flower stickers in your locker.

The key to successfully using your locker is to keep it organized. As mentioned, putting shelves (you can get them at Wal-Mart or Target) in your locker is one way to better organize things, so everything isn't in one huge pile. If you have trouble organizing your locker, ask your resource room teacher or school counselor to help you organize. There are also several websites that provide organizational tips:

- http://www.cliffnotes.com/WileyCDA/ Section/Organize-Your-School-Locker.id-310989,articleId-53841.html
- http://www.goteeniebopper.com/organize-school-locker.html
- http://www.wikihow.com/Organize-Your-Locker-in-Middle-School-(Girls)

Getting your locker organized in a way that works for you will make your school life much easier. But even after you have your locker organized, you may need extra time to keep it that way. Either get to school early or stay late once a week to put things in order. If you can arrange to keep a set of textbooks at home, it saves a lot of trouble in terms of remember-ing to carry books back and forth every day.

Gym lockers. You will also get a gym (or P.E.) locker. Chances are you will share this locker with another girl. You more than likely will not use this locker for anything more than storing your P.E. clothes and maybe deodorant, a hairbrush and ponytail holders.

This is your call, but you might also want to keep tampons and sanitary pads in your gym locker in case of an emergency. I chose not to, and instead keep a small pouch in my backpack for emergencies. My backpack is always with me when I go to gym because it is too big to fit in my normal locker. If you are lucky enough to have a big locker where you can store your backpack, I recommend keeping a small pouch of tampons/pads in your gym locker. Extras are usually also kept in the nurse's office.

Gym lockers are rarely decorated. There are usually mirrors in the locker room. While it may be tempting, be sure not to stare at every other girl in the room while they change. It's not important what color underwear someone is wearing, or if they are wearing a bra or not. You'd feel weird if someone stared at your underwear. Just change quickly and get ready for class. Your coach will be happy you are speedy.

Like your normal locker, this locker will have a combination lock on it. The combination to this locker isn't crucial to memorize – if worse comes worse, your locker mate will probably know the combination and be able to open it for you since she's more than likely also in your gym class.

Chapter 1

 For all three years in middle school, I had both a regular locker and a gym locker. In sixth grade, I only had a gym locker. The only thing I kept there was a pair of gym clothes and deodorant. Early in the school year, I took my gym locker's lock home to practice on because I'd never used a combination lock before. My dad showed me how to use it; then he locked it on a shoelace and I was supposed to get it off. We did this three or four times, and then I felt comfortable using combination locks. In seventh grade, I had a regular locker for the first time. I decorated it with a mirror, a pen/pencil holder and a bunch of stickers.

Usually lockers are stacked in columns of three or four. Luckily I had a middle locker, so it was easy to reach and open. In eighth grade, I got a bottom locker. This meant I had to bend down on my knees to open it; my fingers would slide because my knees hurt, which made it harder to open the lock (not because I didn't know the combination). I didn't decorate my locker in eighth grade since I didn't use it very much because all my classes had class sets of textbooks and extra copies of the books in the library. My notebooks were light enough to carry in my backpack that year.

A Teacher's Perspective

Sometimes it gets pretty crowded if you have a locker in the middle. If you are bothered by tight spaces or other people standing right next to you, you can ask the office if they can switch you to a locker on the end. This will give you more space to open your locker and take things in and out.

If you are struggling with all of the books and binders and trying to get to class on time, try using a large three-ring binder and have folders or tabs for each of your classes. You can also ask the teachers if you can keep your materials or books in their classrooms. A lot of schools have textbooks online so if you have Internet access at your house, don't worry about taking those huge books home. If necessary, you can have a locker location designated in your IEP.

Advice From Other Girls on the Spectrum

I don't like using a locker at school. Everyone crowds around at the same time, bumping, yelling and slamming their lockers shut. It makes me feel over-

Chapter 1

whelmed. By the time I'd get my stuff and go to my class, I had a hard time settling down and doing my work because I was all shaky and distracted. Knowing this is how I'd feel later, I would get anxious about going to my locker so I just wouldn't go at all. I'd go straight to my class without my books and homework and sometimes I'd get into trouble or get zeros on my assignments.

My resource room teacher noticed this and had the idea for me to have a locker on the end of the row so I wouldn't be squished in the middle. It helped, but the locker area was still too crowded and loud for me. I started carrying ALL of my books with me ALL of the time. To make it easier, my mom bought me a backpack with wheels. My brother said I looked like a dork and teased me about me pulling my "luggage," but I said didn't care what he or anybody else thinks! I decorated it with all kinds of animé patches, and it turns out a lot of kids say it's cool and ask me where I got it. Instead of putting it in my locker during lunch, I stop by the resource room and "park" it. There's also a shelf where I can keep extra books if I want to and a place to hang my jacket.

Some kids might notice I'm different because I don't do things exactly like everyone else. But I don't care because I know I'm *already* different and I'm doing things the way that works best for me so I can get along in the world.

Jessica

Changing Classes

In elementary school, you basically just had your homeroom teacher, and you stayed in the same room all day except for special classes like music, gym, etc. Also, in elementary school, when you went to specials or assemblies, the whole class lined up and followed the teacher to the room where the class or assembly took place.

In middle school, you have many classes, and it is up to you to follow your schedule and get to your classes on time. For most of your classes you have a different teacher, and each of those teachers has different rules you need to follow.

Class periods usually are from forty to sixty minutes long, and you usually have five minutes between classes to get to the next class. It's your responsibility to get to class on time – and have everything you need. Sometimes this is hard when you have to pack up your stuff in one class, people are talking all around you and there are crowds in the hallway to pass by. But do your best to get to class on time. If you have a hard time remembering what to take to each class, ask the teachers or your parents to help create a checklist of the supplies that you need for each class and tape it to the inside of your locker.

Chapter 1

Lunch

If, on the first day of school, you look around the lunchroom and at first don't see a familiar face, try to find someone from one of your classes that you saw earlier in the day. Approach the table he or she is sitting at and say, "Hi, I'm ____. I'm in your whatever-class. What's up?" Then see where the conversation goes and try to join in briefly. You could always talk about the class – or popular movies, music, television shows, actors or books. I've made many small-talk conversations just on the *Twilight* books (by Stephanie Meyer) alone, because so many girls are somehow obsessed with it. It's always a good conversation starter.

Some kids have a Circle of Friends. Circle of Friends is a group of kids who understand you and spend time with you during the day. You might sit with your Circle of Friends at lunch or walk with one or two of them during passing time. They may also sit by you in class or study hall and work with you on group projects.

In most middle schools, you have to wait in line in the cafeteria and ask the lunch lady to put certain foods on your tray. Always say "please" and "thank you." Most people under-appreciate the lunch staff, and the staff always are thankful that you are kind to them.

Don't push or cut in line. If someone cuts in front of you, let it go. It's not worth picking a fight over. If it continues to happen, talk to an adult – outside the cafeteria – about it. That kind of behavior is a form of bullying and cannot be tolerated.

If your school allows you to bring your own lunch, you have it made! You can bring whatever food you like and bypass the lunch line. Always bring an extra snack to share with your friends. Gummy bears are usually a popular treat.

While we're on the subject of lunch, here are some reminders about general manners.

1. Try not to chew with your mouth open – this can offend people.

2. Don't chew and talk at the same time – no one wants to see half-eaten food flying out of your mouth, and you could possibly choke.

3. Use a napkin to wipe your mouth so the crumbs aren't stuck to your face all day. It is also a good idea to check your face in a mirror after lunch.

4. Don't forget to clean up after yourself at lunch – throw away your trash, or if you're getting school food, put your tray back with the other dirty trays.

In sixth grade, it didn't matter who I sat with, because there were eighteen sixth graders and all eighteen of us were in the same lunch period. We all got along pretty well, because we had known each other since first

Chapter 1

grade. We formed a girls' table and a boys' table. Some of the kids liked sitting with the older kids and were allowed to do so. This situation was not typical of most middle school lunch scenarios, because I went to a small private school.

This all changed in seventh grade. I was the new kid and entered a lunchroom with 125 people at one time. I didn't know anyone. I became part of a group of kids at one of the tables because they were the most welcoming towards me. Unfortunately, I had nothing in common with them. But I stayed with them because I was quiet and shy, and too scared to sit with anyone else. I had friends in other classes whom I could have sat with at lunch, but I felt scared to approach them.

I later realized it would have been a better choice to sit with the kids I was friends with in other classes. At the end of the year, some of those girls came up to me and asked me why I never sat with them. I guess I had totally misjudged the situation. I hope you can learn from my mistake and take some chances so that you don't get stuck with a group you don't particularly care about and have nothing in common with.

In eighth grade, I was the new kid once again at another larger school. The lunchroom was not as bad as the one in seventh grade, because it was smaller and there were not as many kids in there at one time. I met one girl who tried to introduce me to all of her friends. This was a nice thing for her to do, but her clique excluded me from conversation because they were "lifers" (they had all been going to this school since first grade and had been tight ever since!) and frequently talked about the "good old days" of elementary school. I had nothing to add to their conversations, because we had no history together. I felt out of place and uncomfortable.

Because nobody in that clique was friendly to me after the first three months into the school year, I developed the "sit-outside-and-support-the-student-store" plan. I'd get myself a bag of Skittles or a pouch of Pop Tarts from the student store and work on homework that I hadn't finished the night before, or work ahead, while sitting by myself.

While I was able to get some work done this way, it wasn't the smartest of ideas to sit by myself, because I didn't have any friends or people to talk to, or to even ask for help on homework. We weren't allowed to bring lunch, so you either had to endure the lunchroom or do what I did. I wouldn't recommend doing what I did. The best scenario is to try and be social, make some friends and enjoy the forty-five minutes away from class and teachers.

A Teacher's Perspective

The lunchroom can be especially hard for students who are bothered by loud noises, smells and commotion. At some schools, the counselors or other staff have lunch groups (sometimes called "Lunch Bunch") or other options for kids who have a hard time in the lunchroom. They may also have a lunch group for new students, girls only or groups based around a specific topic. Lunch groups are a great way to get to know other kids in a smaller and quieter setting.

Sounds and Other Things That Can Make You Go Crazy

It's eight in the morning, and it is the start of the school day. The bell rings. The ringing annoys your ears. Guess what? Typical people hate the bell too but probably not as much!

Other sounds to deal with in the classroom that could really drive you crazy are the fluorescent lights humming, the chalk scratching on the blackboard, the kid next to you tapping his fingers on his desk, etc.

I found that the best strategy for dealing with all these distractions was to sit in the front row and concentrate on what the teacher was saying and writing on the board. When you sit up front, the classroom distractions are usually in the background and at least out of sight. You may also want to talk to your teacher about working in a private area, wearing earbuds, etc., as ways to get away from distractions in class.

Also, during the first few days of school, you will experience your first fire drill. Talk about loud! Fire drills are conducted to make sure the school's alarm systems work and for students, teachers and other staff to practice evacuating the building, etc., in case of a real emergency. There are fire alarms all over the school; they are usually red with a bright white light. They make very loud beeping-type sounds, and their lights flash brightly.

You've been through the drill before, so remember how you dealt with it in the earlier grades. Don't be scared – there isn't an actual fire. But you need to learn what to do in case there would ever be a fire or other school emergency.

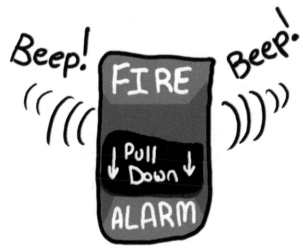

Chapter 1

You will be told to leave all of your stuff in the classroom (don't worry: nobody will steal your stuff) and follow your peers calmly to go outside of the building. Stand quietly and wait for a teacher or administrator to tell you it's okay to go back to class.

In my school, the school day begins at 8:00 a.m. At this time, the bell rings and that means you should start getting to your first period class (most schools give you five minutes to get to class). This may be different at your school though, so check it out.

On the way to class, there may be kids who bang into you in the hall. Try to stay cool and don't hit or push back. In most cases, this is an accident, as the hallways and walkways are crowded with kids rushing to and from classes. There are also many sounds, such as lockers closing, kids screaming at each other, doors opening and closing ... you get the idea. There's a lot of action at one time. If this bothers you, you could put your iPod or music on since your headphones could block out just about everything.

One of the big things you must realize about middle school kids is that some kids hug you a lot. Hugging is supposed to be a way of showing that you care, or that you are happy to see someone. If you don't like to be touched, try to explain this to your friends and suggest they do something else instead – maybe they could nod at you, wink, smile, give a high five or a virtual high five. Never go up and hug a kid you're not friends with.

I was never bothered by loud noises, so fire drills and kids talking loudly wasn't a huge problem for me. However, if sounds like the bells ringing bother you, you could bring earplugs – it's okay! Some of the kids in middle and high school who don't have ASD do it too, because the bell is also annoying to them. Other options are to bring your iPod with headphones and block out all the sound with your favorite music. What could be better?

A Teacher's Perspective

Fire Alarms – Be sure to ask the principal if iPods are okay to have in school. If you are bothered by fire alarms, you can ask the teachers or principal to let you know ahead of time if they are having a drill.

Fluorescent Lights – If there is a window in the room, try to sit by it. You'll be able to get more natural light and you won't notice the fluorescent lights as much.

Hallways and Transitions – The hallways in middle school can be extremely hard to maneuver, especially if you don't like it when someone accidentally bumps into you. If the transition between classes becomes too much for you to handle and is a huge source of anxiety, ask your teachers if you can leave thirty seconds to a minute early to get to your locker before the craziness hits the hallways.

Advice From Other Girls on the Spectrum

I HATE fire alarms. When I was a little kid, I'd completely freak out if it went off and crawl under a table. I wouldn't follow instructions, and one of the adults would pull me out against my will and carry me out. It made me really upset.

Eventually, I got too big to be carried out, so they tried talking to me, insisting, demanding I come out from under the table saying things like, "If it was a REAL fire, Mattie, you would get burned if you don't leave the building!" But that scared me and I'd cry, and then somebody would yell at me and that only made it worse!

My mom talked with me over and over again about it, and so did the other adults, but I just couldn't THINK when the fire alarm went off because I was too scared.

In sixth grade my counselor, Mrs. Jamison, had some new ideas. She helped me create a plan for escape in case of a fire alarm, which I drew myself. It has arrows pointing the way to go. We wrote out all of the steps for what to do. We photocopied it and gave it to all of my classmates, too. Our class practiced the plan even when there wasn't a fire drill. We did it once a week.

Then one day my classroom teacher Ms. Kerry said, "Mattie, there is going to be a fire alarm practice today during third period," and she marked it on my schedule so I could see when it was going to happen. At first I was anxious, but she reminded me that I know exactly what to do. Then right before the alarm went off, she reminded me again that it was going to happen and that it was almost time. So when it did, I was prepared. It was still loud, but it didn't scare me as much. I was surprised that I was able to stay calm, and I guess it's because I knew what to do! I went right to my place and reminded the other kids what we were ALL supposed to do. When we walked in the hall near the alarm, I had to cover my ears, but some of the other kids did too because it's REALLY, REALLY LOUD. I was so relieved to get outside. Ms. Kerry came over and whispered in my ear, "I'm so proud of you, Mattie! You are such a good leader!" All year my teachers warned me when there was going to be a fire drill and would remind me right before it was going to happen so I'd be prepared.

Chapter 1

At the beginning of seventh grade, Mrs. Jamison
helped me make a plan for my new classroom, but
I said I didn't need to show it to all of the kids, I just
wanted to know for myself. She said that was okay.
After the first practice, I told my new teacher, Mr.
Johnson, "I don't want you telling me when the alarm
is. I think I can do it just like the other kids." When the
alarm went off the next time, I did what I always did. I
went to stand in line with my classmates and followed
instructions for going outside and standing where I
was supposed to. After taking roll, Mr. Johnson came
by and high-fived me and my friend, Annie. "Way to
go, following the plan, girls!" he said. I felt really good
about how I was now able to manage fire alarms!

Mattie

Chapter 2

The Kids

 lthough in the end there are more similarities than differences between kids, kids with ASD often have different interests and different challenges than their typical peers. For example, some of my typical-kid friends are good at asking other people for help, while I'm good at public speaking. They're not good at public speaking, and I'm not so good at asking other people for help. Many girls are interested in makeup and boys in middle school, while many people with ASD have different interests, such as video games, animé or their special interests.

Before being diagnosed with high-functioning autism, I always thought that either I was the weird one or that I was the only normal one and everyone else was weird. I always felt different – I never knew why, but I felt like I didn't fit in with the other kids. Our interests were completely different. One girl would go off about how she wanted to flirt with boys on the football team, but I was interested in talking about music or my favorite animé.

Middle school is a tough time for everybody! Your best friend from elementary school might now be hanging out with the weird boy she told you secrets about in fourth grade. Many girls start wearing makeup, talking about boys and wanting to spend three hours on the phone every night. Ironically, the boys seem to be getting less mature.

Everybody is changing, including you. You will meet new people and make new friends who have similar interests. It may take some time, get a little bit lonely along the way, but good things come those who wait.

More on friends in Chapter 5.

New Slang

Until you get to middle school, you are probably not interested in knowing the latest slang words. This is an area where you're mainly on your own, because you're just expected to pick up on it and nobody usually explains it to you.

To help you out, here are some key phrases preteens and teenagers often use. If there are other things you need defined, you could go to www.Urbandictionary.com and look up new terms you hear. Also, watching current TV shows and movies for young people will give you a good idea of the kinds of words kids use today.

The following terms and expressions are common around my school. They are not necessarily the same in every part of the country, so ask around and pay attention to the terms kids in your area use:

'Rents – This term is used to refer to parents, not paying rent on a house.

24/7 – 24 hours a day, 7 days a week.

411 – Give me the information.

Beast – Being really good at something, not an ugly creature from a monster movie.

Bling – Used about jewelry and things that are sparkly, glittery and showy. Think of rhinestones, crystals and diamonds.

Chicks – Refers to girls/women.

Chill – This does not mean being cold, but to pass time and relax.

Dawg – This isn't referring to the dog your family may have, but a friend or someone cool. This term is typically used by boys.

Dope – Your parents may think this means drugs, but today it actually means "cool."

Down-low (DL) – To keep something a secret.

Emo – Coming from "emotional," this term usually refers to a genre of music that is rock but is depressive. It also refers to a dressing style with lots of black, makeup, and being sad and quiet.

Fail – The word still has its meaning as a verb, as in failing a test, but now it is also an adjective, meaning something really "blows." Example: "Oh, that skit we performed in English was fail."

Fo Shiz/Fo Sho – This one just means *for sure.*

Ghetto – It bothers me when people use this word, since it really has a serious meaning. People today use it to mean things like gangster, which is more of a physical fad and looking a certain way. Example: "That is so ghetto."

Glomp – To hug lovingly but not sexually. This happens all the time, it's almost like a tackle hug.

Homeboy – Also called "homies." Homies/homeboys/homegirls are your friends.

Hot/Hawt – It may be warm outside, but this kind

of hot/hawt isn't about the weather; it means attractive.

Murk – I'm not sure where this one originated, but it means to beat someone severely. This is used around my school mainly when talking about sports teams, especially cross country. Example: "Our football team is going to murk the rival school's team."

Owned/Pwned – This isn't to own someone like you own a new game, but it means to be really good at something.

Reeks – Smells bad.

Sick – Means something is awesome or great.

Social suicide – This is something you hear a LOT. It is used when you make a move or do something that is considered stupid by your peers and can result in you having no friends.

Stoked – Very excited about something.

The Bomb – This means that something is great. Be careful how you use this term. Schools may take saying this seriously because sometimes there are bomb scares. "That new show is the bomb."

Tight – This doesn't mean your jeans don't fit but that you are good friends with someone. Example: "Alice and I are tight."

Tool – This isn't a hammer or a nail, but today it is used to refer to a not-so-smart person. Usually a tool is made fun of.

Trashed – This doesn't mean someone threw something out – it means you're drunk.

Two cents – This does not mean two pennies. It means that you are adding your opinion to a conversation.

Wangster – Wannabe gangster.

Yo – Even though originally a Spanish word meaning "I," in English it is now a way to say hello.

The following terms are sexually related. You should be especially aware of their meanings to avoid misunderstandings.

Bang – To have sex.

Hookup – To be dating/having sex with someone.

Knocked up – When a girl is pregnant.

Player – Someone who dates a lot.

Slut – A girl who sleeps around or dresses a certain way that your parents most likely wouldn't approve of, such as short skirts, high heels, low-cut shirts, heavy makeup.

The bases – This is a way to describe "how far" someone has gotten sexually in a relationship. First base is usually known as kissing, second base is touching someone's chest area (usually a girl's), third base is touching lower private parts, and a home run is having sex.

Swearing in middle school is fairly common, but most kids are smart enough not to do so in front of teachers and other staff as that would more than likely get you in trouble. If you don't like your friends swearing, try to ignore it, walk away or get other friends. You don't want to cause any fights or arguments for being a "goody-two-shoes," and you do not want to be bullied later on. (I don't have enough fingers to count how many times certain people said the F-word in my school.)

I watched movies such as *Mean Girls*, used online slang dictionaries like urbandictionary.com and asked my friends to explain the meanings of obscure slang words. Your friends will want you to be part of their group and understand their "language," so they will help you learn new slang.

Do not use most of these words in the classroom or with adults – they are just for your peers and friends. In many cases, it is best never to use slang, but just to understand the words when you hear people using them. I try not to use many of them – I maybe use one or two in conversation with my friends.

The lunchroom and the hallways in between classes is typically where you'll hear slang or swearing. When kids notice that teachers or adults are around, they whisper when they swear or say certain slang words.

If you don't feel comfortable asking other kids what certain slang words mean, you can ask the counselor or a teacher that you feel comfortable with. Teachers and adults in the schools hear a lot of slang, so they typically know what it means. If you have to ask teachers or adults, be sure to ask them in private or after school when other students are not listening.

Advice From Other Girls on the Spectrum

I don't like it when people use bad words. If I don't understand what the person is saying, I look at others in the group and see how they are responding. If I don't know how to act, I think it is best to do nothing and ask an adult I trust later what that word or phrase means. My parents tell me that there isn't any shame in not knowing something – especially because THEY don't know everything either! I can also ask my cousin, Kathryn, who is older than me, because she knows things are hard for me to understand and she'll explain it. I also ask her if it's something that can be only said to other kids or adults.

One time someone said, "You're a _____" (bad word) and I laughed because I didn't know what it meant. Then I said it myself really loud and got into trouble from the substitute teacher. She said, "Carrie! That's a very bad word. I'm going to write a note home to your mother and ask her to talk with you about your language." This was really confusing because I thought my language was English, was that person speaking another language? Luckily, my mom doesn't freak out over stuff. My regular teacher writes notes home to my mom or emails all the time and it doesn't mean I'm in trouble; it just means that she is trying to help me.

Carrie

Chapter 3

Teachers and Other Important Adults in School

ver the years, my mom and I have sorted and classified my teachers into specific types: hand-holders/warm fuzzies, strict teachers, teachers who are nice but can't teach, "mean" teachers, etc. Since you have a different teacher for every subject, you need to be prepared for many different personalities and teaching styles. Always remember: Teachers are people too – they all have good and bad days, just like you.

I personally enjoy having strict teachers, because they tend to keep the class under control, are very organized, limit distractions and usually don't allow bad behavior, cell phones ringing during class, cheating, etc. But it is always nice to have a hand-holding kind of teacher, the one who helps you with everything, understands you and makes things easier. If you have mean teachers, it's best to stay quiet and not get in their way. You don't want to pester them or ask any unrelated questions.

There are advantages and disadvantages to each type of teacher. The most important thing is to know which type of teacher you have so that you can make it work for you.

How to Talk to Teachers

To make your year successful, you should know how to talk to your teachers. First off, never swear or use slang language when talking to them. Always be polite and say "please" and "thank you," and never ask teachers personal questions such as how old they are, if they are married or if they have kids.

Most teachers want their students to do well even
though it doesn't always seem that way. You need
to decide which teachers are willing to help you and
which ones are not so helpful. If you are having any
sort of problem in a class, whether it is social or academic, it is a good idea to set up a private meeting
with your teacher before or after school. If the teacher
is unwilling to meet with you, talk to your parents and
have them call the principal or a counselor and set up
a meeting. If your problem is schoolwork related, such
as if you fail a math test, it is in your best interest to
arrive at school early or stay late and ask that teacher
to review the problems you got wrong on the test.

Other Adults at School

On any school campus, there are lots of important grownups other than your teachers. There are the
people in the office: usually a secretary-type person
who manages when parents sign kids in and out to go
to doctor's appointments or if they are running late one
morning and things like that. Also inside the office is
the principal (some schools, like mine, call this person
the dean). The principal is in charge of everything pretty
much and usually sees the kids who get in trouble. You
want to know who the principal is, but you don't want to
end up in his or her office for the wrong reason.

The most important non-teacher on campus in my
opinion is the guidance counselor. This is a good person
to know. The guidance counselor is someone who talks

one-on-one to students and helps sort out academic and social problems. If you need somewhere to go, someone to talk to, need advice or have questions regarding certain teachers, the guidance counselor could be your "go to" person. Try to meet the counselor at your school in the first week or two of school to introduce yourself, or ask your parents to talk to him or her about any issues or concerns you have.

Among the many areas where guidance counselors can support you are social skills. For example, the counselor can pair you up with an older buddy if you need help navigating around school. He or she can also give you advice academically if you are having problems with a particular subject and/or teacher.

Don't be embarrassed to see the guidance counselor. He or she may become one of your best allies on campus, and if you need a place to go and relax because you are stressed out or you need a break, you are almost always welcome in the guidance office.

> Some schools don't have guidance counselors. They may have advisors, social workers, or homeroom teachers who can provide you with this kind of help.

I would never have thought to go to the guidance office on my own, but in the first week of eighth grade I had trouble adjusting to one of my teacher's styles, so my mom made an appointment to talk to the guidance counselor about my diagnosis of high-functioning autism. After that, I found that the guidance counselor's office was a good place to go if I needed anything.

I used to hang out in the school office before the end of the day to work on homework or on the yearbook. I eventually became friends with the secretary. Every time I entered the office, she would call me her BFF (Best Friend Forever). The people in the office were excited to have my company every day at the beginning of the school year. Sometimes they'd let me help deliver things, staple papers or do other odd jobs if I had no homework left or they just needed an extra hand. I felt special.

A Teacher's Perspective

As Haley wrote, most teachers want you to succeed and do well. Sometimes it's helpful to the teachers if you have a meeting before school starts to talk to them about things that you may need. If you have an IEP, it is a good idea for you and your parents to talk with your new teachers. Your IEP has valuable information in it, like accommodations you may need to be successful. It is important for you to be familiar with your IEP.

General Rules in the Classroom

There are certain rules that need to be followed in the classroom, no matter what kind of teacher you have. Basic rules that many teachers have include:

1. *Be in your assigned seat and ready to work when the bell rings.*
2. *Bring required books and materials to every class, unless told otherwise by the teacher.*
3. *Listen and stay seated when someone is speaking.*
4. *Follow directions the first time they are given.*
5. *Turn assignments in on time.*
6. *Treat everyone and their property respectfully.*

Asking questions in class is important if you don't understand something. Besides, there are more than likely other kids who have the same question as you but are too nervous to ask it. However, there is such thing as asking too many questions. The same is true for answering the teacher's questions. Even if you know every answer, try to let other kids answer questions, too. If they don't get the answer right, then keep your hand raised. If your teacher calls on you, you may answer the question. Don't scream the answers out loud or make fun of someone if he gets the answers wrong.

Also, be aware of rhetorical questions – questions that teachers often use for emphasis but that you are really not supposed to answer out loud. For example, the teacher may be frustrated that students in his class are talking and running around after the bell rings. When he says, "How often do I have to tell you to sit down and be quiet once the bell rings?" he is not expecting a reply but is emphasizing that he is getting tired of reminding the students of proper classroom behavior. If you were to give a literal response, for example, "Ten times," you would be considered rude.

Otherwise, one of my math teachers always said, "All questions are good questions," so keep that in mind, and don't be afraid to ask. Try not to ask a bunch of questions at once.

 I am usually quiet in class. I try my best to pay attention and see if I understand something. A good way to know if I understand is through the homework: If it makes sense and I am able to complete it easily, then I know I understand. If an entire assignment makes no sense to me, I try to go to a teacher's review session for help, ask my parents or ask a friend who does understand it.

Going to teachers' review sessions before tests is also a good idea, since they typically give an answer to a question and then say, "By the way, this will be on the test." Only you and whoever went to the review session will know.

When I know the answers to questions in class, I raise my hand and wait to answer if I am called on. I don't answer questions in class all the time. Many kids think I am a know-it-all because I do well on the tests, not because I'm trying to show off by answering questions in class. Sometimes it is best not to raise your hand at all, even if you know every answer. People decide you know things, depending on how well you do on the tests. That is when you need to show off what you know – not in the middle of a lecture.

A Teacher's Perspective

Every teacher has a specific way he or she likes to run the classroom. This may mean that something that is okay to do in one class is not okay in another. Most teachers have their rules posted or written down somewhere. Often, they will go over the rules and expectations on the first day of school. If you have trouble remembering the rules in every class, make a "cheat sheet" that you can keep in your binder so it's easily accessible if you need a reminder.

Chapter 3

Advice From Other Girls on the Spectrum

Substitute teachers are tough to deal with. When I was in just one class most of the time, my teacher would let my mom know if she would be gone for some reason so my mom could prepare me. My mom would say, "Mrs. So and So is going to be gone, and Mr. So and So will be there instead." That helped a little.

But now that I have so many teachers, it's harder because they don't all tell my mom when they will be gone. When I walk into a room and see there's a substitute, it makes me scared right away. Unless it's a sub we've had before who knows about my challenges, when I do something that's different than other kids sometimes I get into trouble. Like one time in kindergarten, which was one of the worst days in my whole life because I wet my pants at school and I thought I would die of embarrassment. It happened because when I need to go to the bathroom, I need to go RIGHT NOW; I can't wait. We have a plan with my regular teachers that if I need to go, I only have to let the teacher know that I am going to the bathroom; I don't have to wait. But that day the substitute teacher said, "I'm helping another student, go back to your seat and raise your hand. You must wait to be excused." By that time it was way too late, I'd already wet my pants. I was so embarrassed and ran out of the class and straight down to the nurse's office and she helped me call my mom.

So this is what I still remember when I see a substitute, I think, UH OH, this is BAD NEWS. I'm afraid that I'm going to get into trouble because that person doesn't know me or she's going to do something totally stupid that's going to make me UPSET.

My parents had a meeting at school, and now we have another plan. If the school forgets to call or don't have time to let me know there will be a substitute, I find out from my resource teacher when I check in at the beginning of the day. If things get crazy with the substitute teacher and I'm feeling stressed out, I can go straight to the resource room and do my work there. Most of the time, the subs already know this might happen, and if they don't, I'm old enough to tell them myself, "I am supposed to go to the resource room now." Just knowing I can leave if I need to makes it easier to stay.

Sidney

Chapter 4

ACADEMICS

T he real reason you're enduring middle or junior high school is to learn and prepare for your future in high school and beyond. The main goal you should have in middle school is to try your best and get good grades. These grades determine the classes you'll take throughout middle school and even high school.

Almost every class you take will involve class work and homework. You may also want to pursue your special interest, join clubs or sports teams. There are only so many hours in a day, so how will you handle it all?

Homework Tools

In middle school, teachers assign homework in just about every class. Don't freak out; they're not out to get you or make your life miserable. They want you to get practice on the material covered in class so they know that you understand it (this is especially huge in math). My eighth-grade English teacher always said, "Repetition is said to be the mother of learning," and it helps prepare you for upcoming tests.

The hardest thing with homework is knowing how to balance it and get everything done on a daily basis. Here are some ways you may try:

1. Make sure you understand what the assignment/homework is.
2. Record exactly what you need to do; if you are given a handout with the assignment, read

through it and highlight the important parts and be sure you understand them before you leave class.

3. Bring home everything you need to complete the assignment/homework.
4. If necessary, talk with your teacher about homework accommodations.

Once you are at home and are ready to start, consider the following ways to actually do the homework:

1. Do the hardest things first, then the easiest.
2. Do the easiest first, take a break, then do the harder homework.
3. Do the homework in order of what time you have the classes. That is, do things from the morning classes first, take a break, and then do things from the afternoon classes.

A lot of kids have trouble getting all of their homework done each night. If this is happening to you and you are feeling anxious or stressed out, talk to your parents and teachers. This is not good for anyone.

Tests and Quizzes

Studying for tests and quizzes is important, as they can be very important to your overall grade in a course. The next couple of paragraphs are tips for studying so you could get a good grade on any assessment that comes your way.

To study for subjects like science, history, foreign language and English, it is a good idea to make flash cards. If you want to use flash cards for vocabulary, put the word on the front of the card and the definition of the word on the back. For history, if you need to know dates, you could put a year on the front of a flash card and bullet points of what happened that year on the back of the flash card.

For a foreign language, it doesn't matter how you format the cards. You could put the foreign word on the front and the English word on the back, or vice versa. It pretty much depends on how your teacher does vocabulary tests and quizzes. If he or she provides the English word, put the English word on the front and the foreign word on the back.

Flash cards are portable, so you can use them to quiz a friend on the bus or look through them quickly during lunch or even on the way to class. But be sure to put

them away, out of sight, before the test or class starts, so you and others aren't tempted to look at them in class as that may get you accused of cheating.

If you don't like to write, you can make flash cards online or answer questions on a flash card computer or iPod format. See http://www.apples4theteacher.com/

flash-cards.html for examples of computer flash cards. For iPods, there are applications called FlashMath, Kid-Calc Math Flash Card, Flash My Brain Flash Cards, etc. If you don't have a computer, you can usually find one in the school library or your town library.

The only way to really determine if you know your math is to do practice problems. Most textbooks have answers to the odd-numbered problems in the back of the book, so it's a good idea to do the odd-numbered problems and then check if your answer is the same as the one in the book.

If your math teacher says you can't use a calculator on the test, try doing practice problems without a calculator to get a feel for the test. If you want to take a practice test, ask a parent to choose questions from the book and write them down on a sheet of paper for you to do and for the person helping to time you. While it is true that you have to memorize certain math facts and formulas, learning math requires doing actual math problems.

So you're freaking out now because #22 on the math homework is really hard. What are you to do? You can skip it and beg during first period if any of your friends got the answer. But that would be wrong! You should not turn to copying since you will get in trouble. Instead, you could ask your friend to explain how she got the answer and see her work. Or ask your teacher (resource room teacher). Another option is to ask to go to an extra help session. Your teachers want you to understand what's being taught in class, and they will guide you through your problem since they want you to understand. Sometimes they'll give you shortcuts and other helpful tidbits they don't necessarily share in class.

If you're stuck at home and a parent is not able to help, here are some resources you could use:

1. **Your textbook.** Usually textbooks have a lesson on what the homework problems are and present problems similar to the ones you're unable to do (this mainly applies to English, math and foreign language). There are also online resources you can refer to, such as Dr. Math (www.mathforum.org/dr.math) and PurpleMath (www.purplemath.com).

2. **Your friends.** Some of your friends may understand the homework better than you. Ask if they can guide you through the problem or provide hints, but don't just have them give you the answer. If you're merely given an answer, you won't necessarily understand how your friend got the answer, which is the important part.

> **A quick note regarding extra help**: If you realize you don't understand something the night a homework assignment is given, seek help the very next day, so you do not fall behind. Don't wait until the day of a test or the day before a test. You might be sick the day before a test and you might not be able to attend extra help sessions if offered.

3. **Older siblings.** Though it may have been years since they've seen the material you're covering in class right now, a quick read through the textbook or instructions on a worksheet will likely give an older sibling enough of an understanding to help you. But don't just ask for the answer; ask them to help you understand the work and logic behind the answer so you can do it yourself the next time.

If you are really struggling with homework or schoolwork, don't be embarrassed. It is best to let your parents know so they can talk to your teachers and administrators so you can get the help you need. Maybe you just need extra time or a different teacher with a style that works best for you. Don't settle just because you're too embarrassed to find solutions. Seek help.

Most everybody agrees that studying is no fun. Since there is no way to avoid doing homework if you want good grades, try to come up with a little trick to motivate yourself to study. For instance, suggest to your mom or dad that if you get an eighty-five or above on the test, they will let you buy some of your favorite music on iTunes, a new video game or a new shirt. Because you will want those rewards, you will work and study to try to guarantee you get above an eighty-five on that test. Be creative with ideas, so you can make little goals to work towards. Motivators have always helped me.

Studying isn't one of my strong things. But I am lucky that my memory is great, so I remember almost everything I read or hear. In sixth, seventh and eighth grade, I took notes in class or outlined the lessons with my mom, and then we studied together. She quizzed me on the things I did in class and had to learn for the test. Some kids in my class had problems taking notes, and their teachers would give them a copy of the lesson outline to follow. Some of the kids highlighted the outline as the teacher talked about it.

Something that worked really well for me was that my mom would read my history, science and English books, outline the chapters with me and then I would type them on the computer. My hands hurt easily and I don't write very fast. But I am a much faster typist, so I would take the notes and type them on the computer so that I would learn all the information.

Chapter 4

Another thing we would do was read together and then discuss the main themes and ideas of my English reading books. This helped me because I knew what to focus on. People with ASD are really detail oriented and sometimes focus on the details and miss the key concepts.

Not everyone's parents have the time to help with homework and assignments. If your parents can't help you, you can use some of the suggestions above and/or go online and read *SparkNotes* or *CliffNotes* on books that will help you get through them. *SparkNotes* uses many brief summaries to make it easy. Be careful though – do not plagiarize (copy) and do not use *SparkNotes* as a way to avoid reading the books. You use it after you read a book to make sure you completely understand it. As you read, you can type on a computer if your hand hurts like mind did. Plus, typing the notes helps me memorize.

Another thing I did was to look at studying as if I was memorizing the lines of a script for a play. If you memorize your lines, your performance will be good. So I tried to learn the material almost perfectly, so the "performance" – actually the test or quiz – would be good.

Many of us with ASD have problems with wanting to be perfect. Nobody is perfect – we all have flaws and make mistakes. My mom always says, "Just try your best – that is all we ask of you – you don't need to get 100s. Seeing you make an effort is important."

Most teachers and parents are pleased if they see you trying. If you go home and just play video games all night and blow off your studies, your parents will be less forgiving if you don't do well.

A Teacher's Perspective

Homework is usually a huge issue for middle school students. It is normal to feel overwhelmed and anxious about getting everything done each night. The most important thing is to make sure that you write down your assignments in an assignment notebook. You may need to write down more details about the homework if by the end of the day you have a hard time remembering exactly what to do. For example, instead of writing just "worksheet" for math class, you may need to write down "worksheet – show work on another piece of paper, do evens only." By the time you get home and are ready to work on homework, you'll have all the information you need to get your homework done correctly.

If you have problems getting your homework done at home, check to see if your school has a homework club or a place where you can work right after school. That way if you need extra help, teachers will still be around to help you.

Chapter 4

Haley listed some good resources. There are other resources that can also help you. You can use audio-books (ask your teacher, see audible.com, or iTunes), study guides from your teacher to help you get ready for tests and websites, such as antistudy.com.

Advice From Other Girls on the Spectrum I totally can't do homework. I used to try and my parents would help me, but by the time we were just half finished, all of us would feel like we were going to lose our minds! My dad said (more like sort of yelled), "This is ridiculous! I'm not a teacher; I don't even understand half the stuff they're making her do, how are we supposed to help her?" I cried because I was just as unhappy as he was. It wasn't working out for any of us. I understand most of the work pretty easily, but by the time school is out, my brain needs to rest and think about other things like my special interest of cats.

This year it got a whole lot better because after a meeting at school they changed everything. The only work I have to do now is at school. No homework! I'm pretty quick at a lot of my subjects, especially math and science, but don't really like literature (because we're reading fiction – yuck!). All of my assignments for the week are inside a notebook, including the things that are supposed to be homework. I can do up to one week's worth of work if I like. I'd do more, but my teachers say I need to stay with the class and not get too far ahead.

Literature is hard for me to understand because the teacher asks complicated questions and characters in the stories do things that don't make sense. At my school, a seventh-grade Literature Group meets twice a week during that class period. We read the book in smaller sections individually, and then when we meet we talk about it and fill out the assignment sheets together. This has made it a lot easier for me to understand the books. I still prefer NON-fiction and reading about animals, but at least this way I don't have to read homework books at home!

Chelsea

Time Management

I found this quote in the movie *The Great Debaters:* "Do what you have to do, so you can do what you want to do." This means you should first do all the important stuff like homework, chores, things that you have to do but don't want to. If you do your homework, chores and other things you have to do, you will be able to do the things you *want* to do like play video games, listen to music or whatever you like to do for fun. I try to keep this in mind with almost anything relating to middle school.

Chapter 4

Time management is one of the keys to success in middle school, high school and life. Unlike elementary school, where everything is planned and things are laid out for you – and there is little homework – middle school requires you to manage your time and get everything done on time.

One of the best pieces of advice I can give you is to not procrastinate! Waiting until the last minute to finish projects, studying, preparing a presentation or doing a long-term homework assignment is not a good idea. You never know what will pop up and make things even harder to get things done.

I tend to use my weekends to get ahead with homework, or I read a chapter ahead in books each night in case I can't read one night because of a family thing, or some other unexpected event. Even though weekends should be for fun or a "break," it is a good idea to set aside a couple of hours to get organized for the next week. This makes the upcoming week a lot easier, especially if you know you have a test, a recital, a family outing or anything that could make it harder to fit in doing homework. Here are two good ideas to stay organized.

1. Keep a calendar

Keep a calendar, whether on your computer or posted in your room or other area where you do homework. Write down when test days are, when there are quizzes, when projects are due and things like that. Some schools use special planners that list each day and have areas to write in subjects so you will see at a glance when homework is due, when tests are coming up, etc.

Here is what my calendar from last November looked like. I have a Mac, so I used the program iCal to create the calendar. I sorted things by color: blue was school stuff, green was holidays, red was my friends' and family members' birthdays and the purple-pink color indicated other plans, such as going on vacation or seeing friends. PCs running Windows have a similar calendar program called Microsoft Outlook.

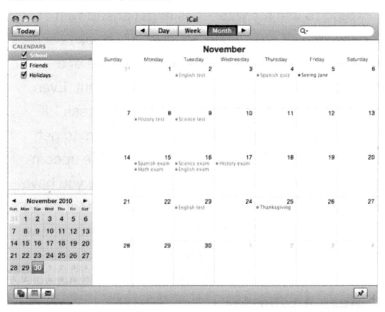

If you don't have a computer, you can do essentially the same with a personal digital assistant (PDA), or handwrite a calendar and decorate it using markers, stickers, etc., if you wish.

Chapter 4

Below is a sample schedule of how to stay organized and manage your time to do everything and still have some time left over to yourself.

On Sunday, think ahead to what's going on the following week. This takes maybe 10-15 minutes. In the sample schedule here, you've got research to do on Monday (let's pretend that research is due the following Monday), a test on Tuesday, a quiz on Wednesday, a project due Thursday and time to yourself Friday night to play video games or whatever you like to do.

Monday – If your research project is due the following Monday, try to get it done before Friday. In this scenario, you want to have Friday night free to do what you like to do. If you get your work done early, you won't have anything stressful on your mind while you are having fun. You should be reviewing for your English test tomorrow (Tuesday) after you finish all of your other homework. Reviewing for the test should take the most time, but it should not get in the way of completing your other homework assignments. Studying for a test is not an excuse not to do homework for another class.

In addition to regular homework, you should begin to look over your math notes to see if there's anything you don't understand. If you don't understand, go to get extra help on Tuesday. This is cutting it close, but better late than never! If you're having trouble with math all along, use your weekends to practice a couple of problems and get extra help on Mondays. As mentioned earlier, you can also look online at sites such as Dr. Math (www.mathforum.org/dr.math) and PurpleMath (www.purplemath.com) to help you out if no one else can give you a hand.

Tuesday – This is the day of your English test. You should have studied the Friday before and glanced over your notes for a few minutes as a review over the weekend. You have to study for your math quiz and do all of your regular homework. If you still have time, do a little bit more work on the project that's due Thursday.

Wednesday – Math quiz. If you had time on Monday, you could have done a couple of practice problems. Look over your notes on Tuesday, and if you need to, ask for extra help. Do not go to extra help the day of a test. It is always crowded, and you won't get the time and attention you need.

Thursday – Your science project is due. You have had over a week to do it. Whatever you do, do not decide to stay up until eleven o'clock Wednesday night trying to finish it. You will be tired the next day and your project likely won't be as good as you had hoped because you rushed. Also, if you're sick Wednesday, you can't just walk into class saying you didn't do your project because you were sick if you had, say, a week to work on the project. Basic idea: It is good to get ahead.

Friday – Make sure you have no leftover work, because you want to have as much fun as possible and have some private time to do what YOU want to do and what makes YOU happy and have fun. ☺

| | | | January | | | |
Sunday	Monday	Tuesday	Wednesday	Thursday	Friday	Saturday
16	17	18	19	20	21	22
• Work on science project • Review for English test and Math quiz • Do research for History	• Review math problems in case you need extra help. • Study for English	• Finish science project • Study for math quiz	• Science project complete	• Work on history research due Mon-	• My video game time	• Work on research for history

2. Prepare for the Unknown

Life is unpredictable. You might get sick, you might have a dentist appointment right before your math test … and who knows what else. This is what I call the unknown. Of course, preparing for the unknown is like trying to predict who is going to win *American Idol* when the show first starts and they show the auditions. But at least try to get things done in case of the unknown.

Studying in advance, working on projects five days before they are due and doing your homework on a nightly basis is all part of preparing for the unknown. This brings us back to the *The Great Debaters* quote at the beginning of this chapter. Do what you have to do first, and then go have fun, relax and listen to music, play games or do whatever you like to do in your free time.

I think my calendar examples were a bit of a giveaway as to how I stay organized regarding long-term assignments, plans, quizzes and tests. I also prepare for the "unknown" by usually being a night ahead when it comes to studying or reading for school. Being ahead allows me a bit more downtime when I get home each day and gives me more time to study and work on other things. By being ahead, I am able to attend club meetings, spend time with my family, have some free time each day and not be stressed out about schoolwork.

Here is an example of my after-school evening. I usually get home around 4 p.m. I change into something comfortable (usually pajama pants or sweatpants) and relax by drawing or playing video games. Around 5 p.m. my family eats dinner. I take a shower after dinner, and by 6 p.m. I am studying and doing homework, usually until about 8:30 p.m. Then I take a half hour to lay out my clothes for the next day and pack up my backpack with books and homework due the next day. After I'm done preparing for the next day, I take the time to do what I want before going to bed, which is usually listening to music, using my computer, playing games or watching TV.

Most school days start around 8:00 a.m. Some people live far from school, some live close, some take a lot of time to get ready and some don't. Factors such as how long it takes you to get ready in the morning and how far you live from school help determine what time you should get up in the morning. It takes me about thirty-five minutes to wake up, eat breakfast, get dressed, put makeup on and make sure my backpack is ready from the night before. I live thirty-five minutes away from school. Since I take a bit of time to get ready and my dad drives me to school, we leave at 7:00 to avoid rush hour traffic.

This means I get up at 6:00. That's early, especially for me who is not a morning person, but I don't have a choice. If it were up to me, school would start at 10:00 a.m. I like to sleep in. But we can't always have what we want. Wake up on time. Have a parent wake you up or use an alarm clock. Try to eat a healthy breakfast so you will have energy. Then brush your teeth, put on deodorant and get dressed. Then, brush your hair and style it if you want to, and put makeup on if needed.

A Teacher's Perspective

If you struggle with long-term projects and waiting until the last minute, ask your teacher and/or parents to help you break up the project into smaller parts to do along the way. If you work on it piece-by-piece, it will help reduce your anxiety and you will end up with a much better project than if you rushed to complete it the night before. Make sure to use your assignment book or homework planner to help you prioritize your homework assignments.

Group Work

Sometimes teachers assign projects that require you to work in groups with other students. If you have a Circle of Friends (see Chapter 1), they may be in your group. Your teacher either assigns groups or people go with their friends. If the groups are popularity contests, you may not be chosen. Their loss! Sometimes people choose you because they know you are smart – not because they want to be your friend. Try to be proactive and choose another smart person to work with. If your partner(s) is smart, you will be able to distribute the work more evenly.

Group work is often not fair. To play it safe, make sure to do your part. Don't be quiet in group work and don't let yourself get bossed around. The kids may try to make you do more work than you should because you are smart. If you have to do everything, tell the teacher after class or after the project is due.

A safe way to show who did what on group work is to put your name on everything you did. It shows who did what, and your teacher will know if you did more work. Finally, don't boss around the other kids in your group, telling them that they are stupid and don't know what they are doing.

Group work can be very frustrating. Just remember: Keep your cool, do not cry, yell or freak out. If things get really bad, talk to your teacher alone before or after class. Never yell or hit another student, no matter how frustrated or anxious you become.

A Teacher's Perspective

Working in a group requires flexibility. The topic the group chooses may not be the topic that you want to work on or a topic that you are interested in. That's okay. Try to find something related to the project that you feel you can do successfully. It's important to listen to the other group members. If you get frustrated with the group, feel free to take a quick break (get a drink of water, etc.) and then return to the group. Make sure to ask if you missed anything while you were gone.

Electives

In middle school, you get to take classes of your choice, called electives. When it comes to choosing an elective, take something you feel passionate about like 3-D art, graphic design, creative writing, computer science, etc. Electives are classes you usually take for a grade, but the topic should be fun and have minimal amounts of homework. Electives should be the one class a day you really look forward to.

The Internet

The Internet is a great way to stay in touch with people and get information on just about anything. The Internet can also be great for helping out with academics. I mentioned some academic help sites I've used, such as SparkNotes for English and Dr. Math and PurpleMath for math.

But despite its many advantages, there are lots of reasons to use the Internet with caution, such as people posting pictures of themselves taking drugs, drinking alcohol or being half naked; people posting false information about themselves to fool  people; as well as numerous other scams.

It's confusing, but if you follow certain ground rules, the Internet can be a positive thing:

1. Don't talk/communicate with people online you don't know.
2. Keep your personal information private all the time.
3. Never buy anything online unless you have your parents' permission.

Chapter 4

Reliability of the Internet. Not everything you read or see on the Internet is true. It's like TV – you need to filter out fact from fiction. The Internet is a great hub to find out about stuff, but not every source is reliable. For example, using things such as "John's Website on George Washington" wouldn't be as reliable as your history textbook or an online biography by a famous historian.

Check your sources and confirm your facts by using encyclopedias, comparing multiple sites, and using .edu websites, the latter are usually almost always accurate because they are written by professionals or teachers at universities and colleges, And be sure to give credit to the original authors if you are using their ideas in your research.

A Teacher's Perspective

The Internet can be a great source of information. Most schools have specific resources online that you can access for research papers. Websites, such as Wikipedia, are not recommended for research papers. If you are unsure about what you can use off the Internet, ask your school librarian. He or she will be able to tell you the types of resources your school uses and has available to students.

Clubs and Other Types of Extracurricular Activities

Clubs, unlike electives, meet before or after school and don't involve grades. In clubs, people with similar interests meet and get to know each other and talk about similar interests. Examples of clubs are the animé club, art club, Harry Potter club, political clubs and clubs for various causes like Students Against Destructive Decisions and the Gay-Straight Alliance.

If you join a club, try to attend all the meetings; get a friend to join with you or, even better, try to meet a new friend or two. It is usually easier to make friends in this way since the people who join the club have an interest in whatever the topic of the club is. Therefore, you almost instantly have something in common to talk about. For instance, if you join Harry Potter club, you can ask somebody who her favorite character is, if she disagreed with the ending of the last book or any other debatable topic.

After you get to talk to someone and feel comfortable with the person, ask for his or her IM screen name or phone number and try to pursue the friendship. This is not always as simple as it sounds, but it is a good way to get to know new people. You may find that you have even more things in common!

Try not to dominate the conversations with all that you know about a subject. Take turns and try not to fight about how you feel on the subject.

Chapter 4

If you are in sports or art, for example, don't tell people they are bad at it – even if they clearly are. The thing about clubs is that they are based around hobbies – you don't have to be an expert at something to be a part of it. Don't go telling people they're slow runners or the noses on their portraits look like elephant trunks. Everyone who joins a club wants to share what they know in a stress-free place where others won't judge or criticize them, even though sometimes it can be a good idea to give comments and criticism to help and be supportive.

Clubs are not competitive (except for chess maybe), so don't go saying "my work is better than yours" or anything like that. Manners apply to clubs, too. You don't want to be the only one who isn't really part of it because you say things that others find offensive.

Middle school is a lot of work. It is good to have an outside interest no matter what it is, just so you can get your mind off school and all of its stresses. Participating in clubs and extracurricular activities, whether it is an art class, team sport, chess club, etc., doesn't always appeal to people on the autism spectrum. Let's face it: We've been at school for about eight hours dealing with different people, different sounds, work and the daily social stresses. Sometimes you may feel that you just want to go home and relax and not do anything outside of the classroom. But there is a club out there for everyone: a place to be yourself, meet people with similar interests and talk about them.

The hard part is finding the time to do it all. It's okay to go home at the regular time and do homework, but it's also okay to go to your friend's volleyball game and then do homework. You don't have to do a bunch of extra stuff, but if you would like to get involved, get out there!

During middle school, I took many art electives. I took 2-D, 3-D and graphic art. In eighth grade, I also took art. There are many different electives other than art – I took art because it is something I enjoy and I want to continue learning about. If art is not of interest to you, you can take band, chorus, debate, yearbook, foreign language (in some schools, this is a requirement), or computer science.

In a typical middle school, there is a wide range of clubs to choose from. Because the school I attended in sixth grade was small, there were only three main clubs: The National Junior Honor Society (some schools have an equivalent known as Junior Beta Club), the school newspaper and Student Council.

My sixth-grade English teacher nominated me for the National Junior Honor Society (NJHS). The NJHS was only open to kids who did community service and had a 3.3 GPA (this is about a B+ average in all subjects). The NJHS organized fundraisers, went to retirement homes to help the residents and other things to benefit the community. Because I love to write, I wanted to join the school newspaper; however, it was only open to eighth graders.

At the larger school I attended in seventh grade, there were no clubs other than sports teams and NJHS. My NJHS membership was carried over from sixth grade. Unfortunately, the NJHS chapter wasn't well run, and we didn't do anything the whole year except for a canned-food drive. As I mentioned, my seventh grade year was a bust both academically and socially. The school just wasn't a good fit for me. I felt lost, and was not really involved.

When I transferred schools once again, the focus in eighth grade was on academics, not on extracurricular activities. My NJHS membership wasn't carried over, since the school had a Junior Beta Club and was more academic than service based. I missed getting into the Junior Beta Club by about a point. There weren't many school-based extracurricular activities for me to participate in, so I continued to take art classes outside of school.

A Teacher's Perspective

Electives – Some schools only have a few electives such as art, music, computers, family and consumer science, technical arts and drama. Once you get into seventh or eighth grade, sometimes you can apply to be a teacher's helper or volunteer in an elementary classroom. Talk to your counselor about other options for electives if there isn't anything you are interested in.

Clubs and After-School Activities – The typical day in middle school can be physically and emotionally draining. It's okay to limit the amount of club and other activities you do after school. It is a great way to meet and get to know other students, but for some students it is hard to stay at school that extra hour or two that it takes. Try to find at least one activity or club that you are interested in attending and try it out. You may end up liking it!

Chapter 5

FRIENDSHIPS

Dreams Don't Come True*

All I have ever wanted
Since the first time last year
Was an accepting group of friends
First go around, failure
Second chance, failure once more

A nonconforming soul was born today,
Only to have her dreams shunned and thrown away
Her blind eyes widening to see light, and then
The soul sits at a table of other girls, all who conform
She is friendly, and they don't talk
In fact, they ignore her
She doesn't exist to them
She cries alone, her weeping unheard,
She then wonders why this happens to her
She has a voice, but no one listens to it

The nonconforming soul goes with the girls again
They act friendly to her today, and
Then her blind eyes open wide and
See the masks they hide behind
She exposes their identities and the
Dreams of having loyal friends are shunned

*I wrote this poem at the beginning of eighth grade.

Chapter 5

friends can be classified into different groups. Like Mark Twain, the famous author, once said: "If you have one best friend in your lifetime, you are ahead of the game." This means that most people don't really have a "best friend," so don't feel bad if you don't have true friends at this point. Most people (if they are honest with themselves) have very few true friends. They may have many acquaintances, or people you just say hello to when you see them. This doesn't mean they are your friends.

In addition to friends and acquaintances, there are "frenemies." These are people who may pretend to be friends but are mean and talk about you behind your back. In other words, frenemies are friends and enemies at the same time. These are the worst kind of friends because you can't trust them. To complicate matters, there are also (1) lab partner friends (people you just work with in school, whether or not you like them), (2) friends that you need to tolerate because they are friends with your friends ... and the list goes on.

In my experience, friendships in middle school are messed up in a big way. One day someone is your best friend and the next day the same person is your worst enemy whom you can't even bring yourself to say hello to. For all you know, the boy who sits alone at lunch every day will become the most popular kid in school. It's all so confusing.

For the first few days, it's absolutely cool to talk to whomever you were friends with in fifth grade. But meeting new people is an important life skill, so in this chapter we will look at ideas for how to talk to people and be friendly. It can be hard, but working on it will help you in the long run. No matter where you are, you will always meet people. It is important to know when to be friendly and when not to be. It is also important to know how to start a conversation and when and how to end it.

Something big that you'll see in middle school (especially among girls) are exclusive friend groups made up of several people, known as cliques. Kids who belong to a clique are usually very close-knit and not necessarily open to new "members."

Don't let it bother you if you don't belong to a clique. If you want to get new friends, what has worked for me is to find someone who is in your classes and looks friendly, and then saying, "Hello, I'm ____, you're in some of my classes" and use some good ice breakers, like "How was your weekend?" or talk about something that happened in a class that you are both in. Asking for their phone number or IM screen names helps too. Most middle school girls communicate outside of school, and it is easier because you don't have to make eye contact, or try to read their facial expressions.

Chapter 5

Making Friends

If you are a person who doesn't particularly care about making friends, you still need to know how to address people, because humans have contact with one another on a daily basis, whether it is buying a ticket at a movie theatre, ordering food at McDonald's, making a doctor's appointment, etc.

Talking to people with respect is important. It's okay if you don't want friends, you could just go to school, do your work, be pleasant to the kids and teachers around you and then come home. Just smile and say hello. It gets you a lot farther than you think. You don't have to be a social butterfly, but knowing how to talk to others is half of the battle.

Making friends is not the easiest of things to do, but a few easy "icebreakers," or phrases to start basic conversation with, are good ways to get to know people and have conversations with them.

Here are some questions to start out conversations:

- "How was your weekend?"
- "What is your favorite book/band/place to shop?"
- "Did you read the new issue of *Seventeen* with [whatever movie star] on the cover?"
- "Did you hear the new [popular musician] song on the radio?"

These types of questions are better than to use a compliment type of conversation starter. For example, if you say to someone, "I love your shoes" and the other girl says, "Thanks, I like yours, too," the conversation doesn't go anywhere. It is better to ask a question. That way there is more to talk about and you learn something about the other person's interests, which can be a start of a possible friendship.

Pretend you are a reporter on TV and ask questions to learn new information. But remember, this is not a cross-examination: It is important not to ask too many questions and to allow the other person to ask you questions and get to know you, too.

To have something to talk about, it is a good idea to find out about trends. Watch modern movies, read teen magazines like *Cosmo Girl* and *Seventeen*, listen to the pop radio stations, etc. Know what the latest and greatest is, even if you don't particularly like it. In middle school, being like everybody else is the cool thing to do. (I'm not sure why, to be honest. It just is that way.)

Another great way to make friends and get involved in conversations is to find kids who are outgoing. Outgoing kids always set up the icebreakers, they ask a lot of questions and keep the conversation going. When you answer their questions, they learn about you. Turn their questions back to them to learn about them. Becoming friends with outgoing kids tends to work because they keep you talking and make your life easier.

Also remember that a great way to meet new people, and possibly make friends, is to join clubs where like-minded people meet, as mentioned in Chapter 4. That way, you have built-in topics to talk about from the very start. If you like art and you're in the art club, for example, everyone else in the art club more likely likes art too. There is always something to talk about. Maybe someone in the club likes animé art like you do. Then you really have it made, because you two can talk about something you both like. This is true for any club that focuses on a specific interest.

 When I was in middle school, the big thing was the Jonas Brothers. As much as I don't like the Jonas Brothers (if you're a fan, I don't want to hurt your feelings. I respect that you like them, it's just not my kind of music), I still knew the names of all three Jonas Brothers, what their latest singles were and what they looked like just so I could make conversation about them if needed. I could say, "Yeah, I heard the song 'Lovebug' on the radio the other day. The vocals weren't too great, but the lyrics were cutesy."

Try not to slam something someone else likes a lot. Think of one good thing about the group and one not-so-good thing, as in my Jonas Brothers' example. It is not a good idea to offend someone right off the bat.

A Teacher's Perspective

Friendships in middle school are extremely difficult; not only for girls, but for boys, too. Girls are very worried about their reputation and what other people think of them. One day they may be your best friend and then the next day, they may not pay any attention to you. Boys also worry about what other students think of them. Boys in middle school may act out or say inappropriate things because they want to be cool and popular.

In my experience with middle school students and friendship, the students who find an interest that they can share together (like the chess club, drama, music, or art) are more likely to remain friends throughout the school year.

Advice From Other Girls on the Spectrum

After elementary school, people change ... and not always in a good way. Someone who was your friend last year may not want to be friends with you this year. If your friends change, it's okay. That doesn't not mean you have to change. If you don't fit in with the old group any more, find something you are interested in – whether it is band, science, history, reading, etc. – and start hanging out with those people. Most of the time, they will help you out, and you can talk to them if you need help with stuff of the social aspect or not.

Jamie

Trust

Trust is important in any kind of friendship. The trick is to know what kinds of things you can trust your friends with. Here's a good rule to go by when it comes to telling "secrets": How would you feel if the secret was written on the chalkboard for the whole world to see? How bad would you feel if your friend told everybody that you hated your math teacher and that got around school, and back to your teacher?

Most likely, not only would you be embarrassed, you would also be very mad at your friend, and probably be called to principal's office to apologize for saying those things. You'd have to write an apology to your math teacher saying it was a big misunderstanding and you and your parents would be totally unhappy. So bottom line: Don't burden a friend with a secret. Secrets are a bad idea. Period. End of story.

Girls have a tendency not to be good about keeping secrets, especially if they're related to jealousy, often involving boys. How would you feel if the whole school knew who you have a crush on?

People with ASD are seen as very trustworthy, and we rarely tell lies. This is a very fine quality, but the downside is that we assume that just like us, others are truthful, trustful and trustworthy. And as a result, we are easily manipulated and taken advantage of. Over the years, many kids have told lies and I'm usually the one who corrects them, and then I'm the one who gets blamed for stuff I didn't do, or even know about.

Another word of advice related to telling secrets is NOT to tell secrets over the Internet. It may seem easier because you don't have to talk and it is just writing, but it is not private like it would be face-to-face, or even on the phone. Your friend could send everybody on her buddy list what you wrote. You probably wouldn't like the whole world to know what you wrote to just her, and you can't deny what you say as easily.

Watch what you write, and if you have something personal to discuss, do it on the phone, not on the Internet or by texting.

Chapter 5

 It seemed that each time I trusted anyone with anything, it came back around to bite me – friends, my first boyfriend, etc. Therefore, I had to learn the hard lesson only to trust people with things that I almost wouldn't mind others knowing.

The only people you can really trust with anything are your parents, so make sure to have a good relationship with them. They will always keep your secrets safe and guide you throughout life. Brothers or sisters may not always guard your secrets the way your parents would.

When I have a problem, either socially or academically, I tell my mom about it. This way I can get out my feelings and she will help me figure things out. She is the best support system out there. For example, if a student said something nasty to me, rather that saying something nasty back, I went home and told my mom what happened, and together we figured out a way to deal with it.

Sometimes people with ASD misinterpret things. Maybe the comment wasn't nasty – it might just have been a misunderstanding or disagreement about something. So rather than losing a friend, I tried to keep my emotions to myself and went home and told my mom. This has helped me avoid a lot of stress.

Another thing I did to get advice on weird social

situations was to read the American Girl books such as *A Smart Girl's Guide to Middle School, Help!, More Help!, The Official Friends Book, The Care and Keeping of You, Girl's Guide to Friendship Troubles*, and *The New Moon* magazine.

A Teacher's Perspective

Some students may not feel comfortable talking to their parents about social situations at school. Your teachers, counselors, secretaries and the school principal are usually willing to listen and help when it comes to friendship. Every adult in your school went to middle school at one time and has probably dealt with the same things you are dealing with.

If you have an issue with other students and do not feel comfortable talking to adults about it, you can always write in a journal about your feelings. This can help reduce your stress level and allow you to calm down. Often after you write down what happened, you can look back and see what went wrong, so you don't repeat it a second time. It takes time to build trust between friends and, unfortunately, sometimes you have to make a couple of mistakes before you realize whom you can trust and whom you can't.

Other Girls – Bullies and Other Mean People

Bullies are typically unhappy people who think they're happy when they make someone else miserable. Always remember: The bully is the one with the problems, not you!

Unfortunately, there's a lot of bullying going on in middle school, and often kids on the spectrum are the targets. Bullying among girls is sometimes different from bullying involving boys and can be harder to detect and, therefore, harder to deal with.

The best thing is to try to identify who the mean girls are and stay away from them if at all possible. If they bother you, talk to a guidance counselor, a teacher you trust and your parents. Get help before the problem gets really bad.

I wasn't bullied because I always looked a certain way and appeared confident. Bullies don't like going after people who seem happy. Instead they target those who are alone, don't smile and seem lonely. That's one reason why it is important to keep up on trends, make sure you always say hello and try to smile and look happy, even if you're having the worst day of your life! Looking good and happy is like bug spray for bullies. It keeps them away from you.

There's a very harsh but true way to describe many of the girls you'll meet in middle school: backstabbers. They secretly hate each other, tell their best friends' secrets, try too hard to fit in, etc. I know I sound like I have no hope for people, but it is hard at times to find someone who is nice, trustworthy and caring. I can't stress that enough. When you find someone who seems friendly, you never know if they will hurt you or anything.

I'm not saying that you should ignore people. Be friendly, but keep your guard up and be aware of what you tell people and what they say to you. Mean girls are a common breed. In elementary school, you may have had friends who are boys, but that is not so common in middle school. It's tough because I had more in common with many of the boys than I did with the girls.

 In sixth grade, all my friends who were girls had been my friends in elementary school, so nothing really changed, except for the fact that one or two of them began becoming in-terested in boys. Eventually, most of the girls who chased the boys ended up getting hurt and realized it was silly to hang out with the boys only.

Many of the girls I wasn't friends with began join-ing team sports; volleyball was especially popular. Maybe that's because guys usually don't have their own teams until high school. Joining a team is a great way to get to meet people. It helps if you are good at

Chapter 5

the sport you play. If you are not, it may be better to join a club that isn't competitive.

Personally, I've always been horrible at sports, especially volleyball. I never joined a sports team in my three years of middle school. If you would like to join a sport but don't think you're good at it, I suggest joining a competitive-against-yourself type of sport, such as tennis or swimming. That way, your teammates will not be angry with you if you mess up. Another option is to be a team manager. You get to go cheer at games, keep score, etc. This allows you to be part of the team without playing the sport.

All of that said, sometimes you can make friends when you're not good at a particular sport. When I was in seventh grade, I became friendly with some girls because I was not good at volleyball. This was because in P.E., a couple of them helped me hit the ball, and they turned out to also be in my 2-D art class, so we began talking because we had things in common other than me being horrible at volleyball. They felt good about themselves by helping me learn to hit the ball over the net, and they liked my artwork and I'd show them certain techniques I used to create it. So all of a sudden, we had something to talk about other than tips for hitting the ball over the net. Art class once again came my rescue. What seemed like an unlikely friendship, the artist being friends with jocks, was actually possible, so you never know what can happen.

A Teacher's Perspective

It's a sad fact that there are, and will probably always be, bullies in middle school. Bullying nowadays has gone high-tech with the use of texting and social networking pages, like Facebook. If you are being bullied online or through texting, be sure to report it to an adult you trust or your parents. Online bullying can get spread around quickly and get out of hand. It's important for both you and the adults you have confided in to find a solution to the problem that you're both comfortable with.

Advice From Other Girls on the Spectrum

In elementary school I was friends with Kelsey and Shoshanna, but when we got to middle school things changed and they stopped hanging out with me. One day I went to sit at their table at lunchtime and they didn't leave any room for me. I said, "Hey, can you scoot over?" And Kelsey said, "It's too crowded, Katie, go sit some place else." When I walked away, I'd heard them whispering and giggling. The third time in a row that this happened, it finally dawned on me that they weren't EVER going to make room for me. I heard one of the girls say, "She's weird!" and I couldn't believe it when my friends laughed, too. I put my tray down and left the cafeteria quickly before anyone could see I was about to cry. I didn't understand why they were being so mean to me. I went to the girls' restroom and cried, and when the bell rang I stayed there.

After that I stopped going to the cafeteria because it hurt so much to see my friends not being my friends any more. Instead, I skipped lunch and went to the library. I'd sit far back behind the shelves reading all by myself. I tried not thinking about my friends, but I felt sad anyway. Adults noticed I wasn't quite my-self and my mom tried to get me to talk about it, but I wouldn't. Meanwhile, in the hallway when Kelsey, Shoshanna and their NEW friends would pass by, they'd make faces at me or call me "stupid," "retard" and other names I didn't even understand. One day, someone stuck out her foot and tripped me. I didn't fall, but I started crying and then they said, "You're such a baby!"

I couldn't take it any more and ran to the office and said I wanted to go home. I told the school counselor, Mrs. Howard, everything that had happened. She was really nice and said that it happens to a lot of girls, not just me. She told me that the school was about to start an antibullying campaign and that they were going to teach students it wasn't okay to tease or pick on someone because she is different. I didn't know this until later, but my mom told me that Mrs. Howard called in every single one of the girls one by one and talked with them about why it wasn't okay to behave the way they did and that they cried because they felt so bad.

A few days later Shoshanna's mom called my mom and asked if we'd like to go to a movie with them. Afterward we stopped for ice cream, and while our moms were talking at the next table, Shoshanna suddenly said, "Oh, Katie, I'm so sorry!" and we hugged. She told me that even though she was "friends" with Kelsey and the other girls, they also said mean things to her and she didn't know what to do about it. I told her that she was still my friend and that I'd never call her names.

Right after that, Mrs. Howard started a lunch group with fun activities like watching videos and eating pizza. At first it was just a few of us, but because it's so much fun, now several kids come. Shoshanna and I are friends again, but thanks to the lunch group we also have made a bunch of other friends.

Katie

In elementary school kids tend to be nice to everyone. Once you get to middle school/junior high school, many kids get meaner. People don't get that people with autism don't understand many social rules. So it's not uncommon for them to be picked on because of that.

One kid I know does not understand sarcasm, so almost everyone uses a sarcastic tone with him, knowing he will overreact. He went to the counselor and asked her to help him. The counselor had the teacher explain to the other kids that this was not acceptable behavior. So now he can play along and isn't as hurt by the comments.

Jamie

Boys and Girls

In middle school, your feelings change. Some boys and girls begin taking an interest in each other as more than friends. It's called dating or having a boyfriend/girlfriend. It's okay to have a crush on a member of the opposite sex. It's normal, really. It is also okay not to have a crush on somebody.

Some quick advice regarding your feelings for boys:

1. Many girls who have crushes on boys tell their other friends (who are girls) whom they have a crush on. This is often a bad idea. Think of it like this – would you write, "I have a crush on Joe" on the board in one of your classrooms for everyone to know? If you said no to that, now you understand why you shouldn't tell your friend. Even if it is a "secret," girls tend to gossip about

how they like other guys, or even worse, they try to go after the guy you like.

2. Turn down other girls' offer to talk to a guy you like to see if he likes you back. It could be embarrassing for you if he doesn't like you back, or your friend could end up flirting with the guy.

3. If you want advice on guys, it's best to go to someone who won't tell the world who you like, try to introduce him to you or do anything you think is inappropriate. Your mom, older sister, or maybe even your dad, are great go-to people to talk to about crushes and boys. They always give you the best advice, even though you may not think so at the time-☺

In middle school, dating is generally a bad idea. The boys are usually immature (many are still into potty jokes) and the girls, even if often more mature, have trouble sorting out their feelings. Needless to say, this combination could easily lead to frustration, upset and hurt feelings. My advice would be to have boys as friends for as long as possible before bothering with the new world of dating.

Misconception: Your Guyfriends Are Not Your "Boyfriends"

Being friends with boys is fine in middle school. They can be some of the most honest friends, but they can also be incredibly stupid-acting. Many boys

still think it's funny to scare girls with creepy crawl-
ies and elbow each other for no obvious reason. The
boys who are "mature" tend to be kind to all and don't
do the stupid things such as potty jokes. These are
the guys who can be good friends. Unlike girls, they
don't gossip much and you don't have to talk about
personal female matters.

But be forewarned. Sometimes the immature girls
automatically make the assumption that if you're
friends with a boy, the two of you are dating and "in
love." They might say that your guy friend likes you
in "that kind of way" (this means they think he has a
crush on you). This may be true, or it may not be. If
a boy has a "crush" on you, there are usually certain
signs, such as blushing more, acting overly nice, hint-
ing at a relationship and trying to hold your hand.

Regardless of whether you like each other in a
crush-like way, be careful about pursuing a boyfriend-
girlfriend relationship in middle school. It could end
up ruining a good, solid friendship. You don't want to
lose a good friend because the two of you got bored
and decided "let's date." Once you kiss a boy, things
are never the same with him. As mentioned, personally, I don't recommend dating in middle school at all.
Just develop friendships and keep them, learn from
mistakes and enjoy the company of a guy who is your
friend.

In middle school, I was friends with several guys. In sixth grade, my best friends were guys. I had a girlfriend who would say to me almost every other day, "Haley, he likes you … he called you his girlfriend in math class today," or something like that. I knew it wasn't true that I was his girlfriend, but I did know he liked me in "that kind of way." He always blushed when I hung out with him and stuff like that. It was almost kind of creepy, since he'd deny it to me but never to anyone else. I was not interested in a relationship. I just wanted to continue to be good friends with him.

Try to get to know people outside of school, because then they are more likely to show their true colors. People are either nicer, meaner, or somewhere in between, outside of school. This is because school has rules, which can prevent people from doing and saying things they want to but that are inappropriate. Here's an example of what I mean.

When I was in seventh grade, I was friends with an eighth-grade boy who was a computer geek. Every morning, we would sit outside the building before school started and play computer games, talk about video games, etc. I felt I had a lot in common with this guy, so I eventually invited him to my house. But when he came, things were different. He was very rude to my parents, was bossy, persistent, and everything I

Chapter 5

thought I liked about him at school wasn't there. I had a hard time figuring out why this was. I thought he was possessive as he tried to prevent me from making other new friends. He wanted me to himself, so I stopped hanging out with him.

Around the same time I got "adopted" by a group of "outcast" girls. I was not comfortable with these girls from the very beginning, but I felt that something was better than nothing. That was a big mistake. These girls ended up hurting me more than anyone in the popular cliques could ever have done. Because the outcast girls were insecure, they tended to be mean, gossipy and catty. They all secretly hated each other and everybody else in the school. They had cruel nicknames for every clique, and when one girl was absent, the entire clique would talk about how they hated her.

I knew this was a bad situation for me, but I wasn't sure how to get out of it. I had opportunities to join popular cliques, but I didn't know what I would say to them; I was very shy and felt I couldn't explain why I didn't sit there from day one. These popular girls were socially advanced, and I felt it was too hard for me to fit in. They always had sleepovers, went to the mall together and wanted to date older guys. Some of the girls tried to include me, but I felt out of place because I don't feel comfortable sleeping over at other people's houses, I only eat certain foods, I tend to be shy, and I wasn't interested in boys. So I made the choice of staying with the outcasts and being unhappy there, instead of being out of place with the popular girls.

I had a very hard time "fitting in." I had the general look of the popular girls, but I didn't have the outgoing, bubbly, boy-crazy personality to pull it off. I was more interested in academics, art and video games than makeup, boyfriends and cheerleading. Unfortunately, I couldn't find a middle ground. It was either the popular girls or the outcasts. At the time, I guess I felt "safer" with the outcasts.

In middle school, I had my first crush on someone I saw every Monday at National Junior Honor Society meetings for an entire year. He was very cute, quiet and a popular football player. I never told any of my friends because I didn't want to be embarrassed, and I didn't want them to interfere.

However, someone always asks you who you have a crush on. All I said was that I liked somebody and was working on it. I did not give up the name, so no one could interfere and ruin my chance. By doing this, I fit in because the girls knew I liked someone and it was okay that I didn't say who it was when bugged about it, because I said I was working on it, even though I never did. It shut up the girls, and we'd go on to talk about other things.

A Teacher's Perspective

It's normal in middle school to have crushes on boys your age or a year or two older. Sometimes it feels like that's all you can think about when you get to school.

If there is someone in your class that you like, try not to stare at him or always sit by him. You can say "hi" or give a quick smile if you want, as long as you don't do it several times throughout the day. If you are interested in getting to know the person better, try to find a club or activity that you both enjoy. Go slow and try to become friends first.

Advice From Other Girls on the Spectrum

I'm not boy crazy. Some of the other girls say stupid things about how CUTE this or that boy is. They also care about who is kissing who, who broke up with who and who is going where together. I just don't care about that stuff. My older sister has a boyfriend and I think, "WHY?!!" She used to be fun and play video games or basketball with me, but now all she does is talk about her boyfriend, Brian. Mostly they kiss A LOT. I don't get it, so don't ask me what the attraction is. She also hogs the bathroom more and is putting on smelly lotion and perfume.

I find it really annoying because if you like boys, suddenly you have to worry about how you dress, makeup and things that I don't care about. I know my mom would like it if I dressed nicer and cared about girly things, but my dad says, "Don't you worry about that stuff at all, kiddo; just be yourself! And you don't have to like boys if you don't want to! You've got all the time in the world."

Anyway, I have one friend who is a boy. We play video games together and hang out. He's not as good at basketball as I am, but he tries. He's not my boyfriend, and if he kissed me I'd punch him. I told him that and he said if I kissed him, he'd punch me too, so it looks like it's working out pretty well for now. If you ask me, we're much more of a match made in heaven than my sister and her slobbery boyfriend. I like things just the way they are and plan to keep it that way.

Katelyn

Fitting In

Whether we like it or not, knowing what's cool and what isn't is important in middle school. Reading style and teen magazines, watching current movies, taking note of what other kids are doing and wearing "cool" clothes can be vital to middle school survival.

Chapter 5

Try to follow certain trends unless they hurt you or other people (things like drugs). But remember: Don't make less of yourself to fit in, including ridiculing others even if that's considered cool.

This quote was in my seventh-grade advisor's room, and I would like to share it with you:

"What's popular is not always right, and what's right is not always popular."

If doing drugs and making fun of certain students is what's cool, it still isn't right. Your health or someone's feelings are at stake – drugs are illegal! Everything has consequences, so think about that before acting.

Advice From Other Girls on the Spectrum

I used to be bullied in elementary school. I know I was kind of a weird kid. I like to hum and rock, because, hey, it feels really good.

Over time, I learned it's not socially acceptable to behave that way in public, and now I only do it at home when I'm feeling stressed. Still, even without the "stimming," I am not your average, ordinary kid, and I know it. I'm totally obsessed with my collections. I have several special interests, particularly Barbie. It's not a normal hobby for a kid my age to "play" with Barbies, but I don't play with them, I collect them.

Online there are a lot of people who collect Barbies – most of them adults! There's a Barbie convention every year not too far from where we live, and my mom has taken me to it since I was little. As I got older, I started writing on a Barbie collector forum for kids and young adults where we share what kinds of Barbies we have and post pictures of our collections. I've made a lot of friends this way, and I don't feel so weird any more because to all of these people it's totally normal to be so interested in Barbie.

Other kids in my school also have Barbie collections; one of them is a boy! Wow, if I thought I got teased and felt like I didn't fit in, he has it 10,000 times worse! But to us, Travis is the coolest guy ever on the planet because he can recite Barbie facts better than any of us. We get together at each other's houses every week and talk about our collections, discuss what latest Barbie paraphernalia is available, what new collection lines are coming out, etc. We understand each other really well, and no one in the group thinks any one of us is weird at all! I think other kids could do this with their special interests too – find kids who like the same things you do and you'll probably feel comfortable hanging out with each other.

Kerith

Chapter 5

Parties, Study Groups and More Out-of-School Friendship Stuff

Parties are difficult for me. Sometimes you're invited to parties, and sometimes you're not. It's easy to feel offended and sad if you are not included. I tend never to be invited to parties by kids who claim they are my "best friends."

Even today, I find out people who supposedly are my "friends" are going to parties and hanging out without inviting me. They'll tell me the party they went to over the weekend was great and ask why I wasn't there. The truth is: No one invited me or told me about it! Even worse, people sometimes talk in front of my face about parties to which I wasn't invited before they even happened.

Don't feel bad if you're not invited to parties; sometimes it is a good thing in disguise. Kids may be talking about these great parties, but the truth is that most of them really didn't have fun and wished they had not been invited and that they were at home doing something fun.

If you're invited to a party and you don't feel like going, make up an excuse such as "my family from out of town is here and I have to spend time with them," "it's my grandmother's birthday," "my parents had plans that day," etc. I know lying isn't good, but this kind of "white lies" (minor lies that are considered harmless, and even beneficial, in the long run) are often the only way out of parties without looking like a total dork. Family excuses are the best. Don't say, "I just don't want to go," because you will never get invited and the host will be offended.

If you're at a party and things start getting ugly, refuse to be a part of it. And if someone offers you something you don't want, "just say no" like those anti-drug commercials. Don't let people make you feel guilty if you're not doing something they want to do. If you believe it is wrong, you are more than likely right. Trust your instincts.

If you're at a party where you feel uncomfortable, the best thing is to have a secret pre-arranged code word with your parents. You can call them up or text them your code word. They will know exactly what you mean and come and get you immediately.

As much as possible, I tried to be myself and do what felt best for me. I never wanted to go to any of the parties everybody was talking about, so I was sort of relieved that I was overlooked. That way, I didn't have to make up an excuse for why I couldn't go. At many parties, there were no parents around, and often things went on that I would rather not know about: someone getting drunk, someone smoking cigarettes, people gossiping, people kissing in closets and bathrooms, etc. I would rather be working on my art or watching TV in my own room, or hanging out with my family.

As for using a code word, this is what I do with my parents even if I'm just at a friend's house for the afternoon and I get uncomfortable and don't want insult the friend. For example, sometimes I'm invited to study groups with girls, but no one studies. They just talk about boys, other girls and gossip away. This irritates me after about twenty minutes. I usually try to stay an hour to be social, but then I text my mom to get me out of there. I recommend using a simple code, such as a dog's name, as a way to ask for help in social situations.

A Teacher's Perspective

Having an emergency exit plan like a code word or a password you can text to your parents is a great idea.

Realize that you won't be invited to every party or social event. If invited, try to go to at least one or two during the school year to get to know some other students. It's okay to just go to parties where you know the people that are throwing the party – that's typically the safest thing to do. Feel free to ask someone what is going to happen at the party ahead of time, and if you don't think that it's appropriate or you would like it, use one of the great excuses that Haley suggests.

Social Networking

This area of online communication is becoming more and more popular. Sites like MySpace, Facebook and Twitter are very popular among students in middle and high school. It's a way to stay in touch with your friends, see photos of what's going on in their lives and generally communicate with them. Social networks can be confusing since there are so many different ones, but the most popular right now (at least in my school) is Facebook.

MySpace and Facebook let you have a page and make friends. Facebook is somewhat safer than MySpace, since people have to add you as a friend to see most of your information; it is also more customizable in terms of security. If you've ever used Facebook, think of Twitter as the status updates: A sentence that answers the questions "What is on your mind" or "What are you doing right now."

Some people look at your profile obsessively, without you even knowing, so never post anything that you wouldn't want made public. It's not like talking on the phone to your best friend. Potentially, the whole world could know what you are writing. Once it's in cyberspace, you can't take it back. So be careful with what you post.

Here are some things to think about with regard to social networking.

- *Ask your parents for permission before signing up on one of these sites.* Most of the sites have a minimum age limit of sixteen years old to sign up.

Adults use these sites to get in touch with old friends (for example, my dad has been able to talk to people he hasn't seen since he was in middle school). If your parents already have a site like Facebook or MySpace, they will understand why you might like to have one for yourself.

- *Make your profiles private, so random people you don't know can't add you or find out anything about you.* Every social networking site has options that allow you to do this. On Facebook, there are ways to make it so that people can't even search for you or see your profile unless you add them to your friends list. I used "super lockdown." I never even used my last name, so only people I like and know could access my page. This is important because you don't want to get caught up talking to strangers, which is the danger adults often stress. You never know who is on the other side of the screen. There are pedophiles and criminals who search the Internet for naïve teenagers to befriend. STAY AWAY. These people are very, very dangerous and can hurt you.

- *Decide whom you will add.* Sometimes classmates add you. When I had a profile, I followed the "three things" rule. That is, if I knew three things about someone besides his or her name (examples: you ride horses, your artwork is really cool, you volunteer at the Humane Society), I would add the person to my friends list.

Some kids think social networking is a popularity contest and try to see how many people they can get on their friends list – I know people who have over 500 friends even though they only talk to maybe 25 of them. But in reality, it is not a popularity contest; it's about who you want to be able to keep in touch with, see pictures of, etc., on an online hangout site. Don't get caught up in the adding craze. It's just stupid. No one really cares if you have 2 friends or 1,500.

- *Make photos private ... and appropriate.* People often upload pictures of each other and things they do to these websites. I think this is fun, but make sure you and your friends make the photos private so random people can't get a hold of them. You don't want some creepy, old man looking at your friend's pictures with you in them.

  Also, make sure they are appropriate. A good rule to go by when uploading pictures is to ask, "Would my parents be okay with this picture being in cyberspace?" or "Would I be upset if my teachers saw this?" Your parents might not mind a picture of you and your best friend with sunglasses in the mall, but they will more than likely mind a picture of the two of you in bathing suits at the beach, for instance. The only exception for showing skin is formal dresses.

- *Don't post too much personal information.* Don't use your last name, and post only things that don't matter or won't hurt you (such as you like dogs, you like to hang out with your friends, innocent things like that). There's no need to post things, like where you go to school, what boys you like, where you live or your parents' names (unless they're on your friends list). Besides, if your profile is private and you only add your friends, they should already know most of these things about you and don't need to look at your profile information.

Instant Messaging, Texting and Cell Phones

Many kids in middle school use IM (instant messaging), texting and cell phones to keep in touch with each other outside of school. IM is just like texting, except you use your computer and use either AOL (most common), Yahoo or MSN. IM also has features like video chats, where you can see the other person and talk like you would when you see each other at school every day. Instant messaging is a good way to ask homework questions or things of that sort, but not to talk about your most trusted secrets. Think of the chalkboard example again: Before sending an IM to a friend, ask yourself if you would be offended if the message was written on the board in class. IM with cau-

tion and, like social networking, don't use it with people you don't know.

Most kids in middle school carry a cell phone. Your parents may want you to have a cell phone for safety reasons so you could get in touch with them, the police or anybody else in case of an emergency. But we all know cell phones are completely social. You can play games on them, take pictures, take videos, make videos, search the Internet and call and text your friends.

Keep your cell phone off while you are in class. You don't want your phone ringing or beeping during class, because it is distracting and if people know it's your phone, it's embarrassing and you will get in trouble.

Texting is like IM, except all messages go through the phones. It is NOT free. People often go over the amount of texts their cell phone plans give them and it costs their parents a lot of money, so know your limits on how many texts you get. Another option is to buy a text plan so you don't have to worry about this as much.

Texts are usually very brief – you can't write more than maybe forty words (if you use Twitter, a text message can only be as long as a status update). Usually a status update or "tweet" is about a sentence long. A typical length of a status update/tweet is "Going to the movies." In other words, you can't write an entire essay in a text. Simple messages like "Hey what's up?"

and "Do you have plans tomorrow?" are the basics.

To be able to say what they want without sending a long message, people use a series of abbreviations that are generally accepted in IM/text chat. Some of the slang terms listed in Chapter 2 may be used, too.

LOL – Laugh out loud. People use this even if they don't think things are funny; it's just like a filler if you have nothing to say.

BRB – Be right back.

ROFL – Rolling on the floor laughing (not literally, it just means something is very funny).

G2G – Got to go. This means you have to leave the conversation or do something else.

TTYL – Talk to you later.

ILY – I love you.

U – You.

R – Are.

IMO – In my opinion.

TBH – To be honest.

IIRC – If I recall correctly.

IDK – I don't know.

OMG – Oh my god.

At first, I didn't want to learn text language, but it kind of just happened. In sixth grade, someone wrote "LOL" in my yearbook and I asked what it meant. I thought it meant "lots of luck" since the person was going to a new school the next year and I wouldn't be seeing her much any more. In reality, it means "laughing out loud." That's when I figured out AOL's instant messenger was popular and that terms like LOL were common.

I learned text language from talking to people; some people I know even use it in everyday speech. It's okay to ask people what certain abbreviations mean. That's how I learned a lot of terms the first time. Another way I learned them was from some notepads my mom got me that had all these text-talk things as a checklist with the meanings next to them. I don't use text talk unless I'm trying to be quick with what I'm saying when I text a friend or my parents.

A Teacher's Perspective

Haley is right when it comes to social networking sites ... you can never be careful enough. Be sure to set the privacy settings high on your networking sites so only the friends that you accept can see your information and/or pictures you post. Think of it this way: What you post on your networking site is out in the cyber world and can be found by anyone who really wants to find it.

Chapter 6

Getting Older Can Be Fun – Body Changes

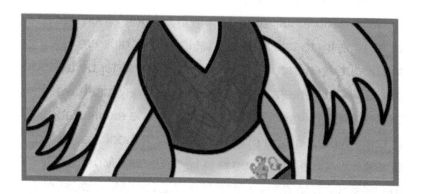

At middle school age, our bodies are changing, and so are our habits. Many girls want to experiment with makeup, clothes and boys, and boys want to play with video games, although some are beginning to show an interest in girls.

Girls with ASD have a hard time fitting in because we tend to mature slower emotionally than our peers. We may not be interested in the latest fashion or makeup craze or chasing boys. We may still like to read *American Girl* books, play video games and dress up our dolls. So, how do we deal with this?

You could still keep your interests, but do them at home and don't talk about them in school. When you're at school, try to talk about what the other girls are talking about even though you would much rather be talking about your interests. For example, you may just have seen the new *American Girl* movie and be excited about it, but a typical group of girls in middle school are talking about how cute Zac Efron is in *High School Musical*. So the best thing to do is watch *High School Musical*, even though you don't like it, so you can be social with your peers and have something to say.

In terms of physical changes, you might be getting taller and noticing other changes in your body: You'll have growth spurts, outgrow your shoes, have to go bra shopping, deal with your period … all the stuff girls rarely look forward to – whether they have autism or not. Puberty happens to everyone. We have no choice. All girls go through the same things. They might start growing at a different time than you, but that's normal.

I'll try to help you deal with the stuff you'll be going through as best as I can.

Mom's Involvement

During the time when your body grows, your mom or trusted female family member (aunt, older sister, older cousin) should be your point person. Seriously, I mean it. Make this adult person your "superwoman." She's been through the same things you're going through, and she will give you truthful advice, unlike your friends who may tell lies about puberty just to scare you. Worse yet, they may be uninformed or mis-informed.

Your superwoman will also help you buy the things you need, be the best friend who listens to you and won't criticize you. It is important that this person is in-volved and is a key part of your life at this point in time.

Throughout middle school, and even now, my mom is my best friend. She prepared me – we would talk about everything from boys to homework troubles; she would comfort me when I was upset, and she would answer any questions I had about anything relating to puberty issues. My relationship with her makes me the person I am today – she is a strong role model and influential figure in my life and always will be.

If you don't have that special type of relationship with your mom, there are great resources out there that you can get reliable information from. As I mentioned earlier, the *American Girls* series book *The Care and Keeping of You* answers many questions and gives you honest information about puberty. Another resource is the school nurse or health (P.E.) teacher or your family doctor if you feel comfortable talking with him or her.

However tempting it may be, I don't recommend relying on your friends because they really don't know either – they are going through the same things you are and could give you the wrong advice.

Your Period

Around a certain time in your young life (maybe as young as nine or ten), you'll start getting your period. Having your period means your body is growing sexually. First of all, every girl, yes, every healthy girl and woman in the world, will have a period. It's a good thing to have your period, no matter how annoying it can be at times. A good book to read about this is Judy Blume's *Are You There, God? It's Me, Margaret*. This book has been around for generations and has helped many girls prepare for and get through their periods.

Chapter 6

This is a time when you might be scared, ashamed or possibly proud. You might be scared since you got your period for the first time without being prepared, ashamed because your clothes are stained and you're the first one of the girls you know to get it, or you may be proud that you got it and the wait is over. The important thing to know is that once you have had your first period, you can get pregnant by having sex with a boy. By sex, I mean intercourse, not kissing.

Do NOT talk about your period and its problems around boys or men. Period talk is for girls only. Never talk about how much blood you lost, how crummy you feel or just about anything else regarding your time of month with the opposite sex or in public places. In case your period starts in class, don't yell out and make it a public announcement. If you can't wait until class is over, ask to be excused to go to the restroom. If you have breakthrough bleeding at school and are unprepared, go to the nurse immediately.

Here are some things you should consider having on hand:

1. **Extra, inexpensive underwear.** In case your flow is heavy, your period comes unexpectedly or you forgot to wear a pad, buy extra underwear that's cheap and can be disposed of if it gets too bloody. Try not to buy white ones because those are more annoying stain-wise. Thongs are also a bad idea if you use a pad, because they won't hold it in place.

2. **Pads and tampons.** You will need them, especially in school. If your friends need them, they'll be thankful you can save them from an in-school disaster or from having to pay to get them from the machine in the girls' bathroom. Your period may not come on time and follow a schedule for a few months, or even years, so it's best to always be prepared.

3. **A little pouch.** This is where you store your tampons/pads. It's a discreet way to carry your "feminine necessities." You should have two pouches: one for your backpack and one for your gym locker so you are prepared at any time of day for an unexpected emergency.

In addition, right before and while you are having your period, wear dark colors on the bottom. This way, if there is an accident, it will not be as obvious. Another good idea is to wear a dark sweatshirt and keep it tied around your waist. If you can, keep an extra pair of dark shorts, pants or a skirt in your locker in case of an accident.

Another important thing you should know about is PMS (pre-menstrual syndrome). People will say if you have this, you are PMSing. Usually this isn't a compliment. When girls PMS, they become cranky and get mad quickly. They may have backaches, headaches or menstrual cramps as well.

PMS usually makes girls want chocolate or other sweets, act out of character or mean, and things along those lines. Know when your friends are getting their periods so you can cut them some slack and be prepared if they're suddenly acting unlike themselves because of PMS. If PMS becomes a serious problem for you, you should talk to your doctor because there are medications to help you feel better.

I got my period before going on a trip to Disney World right before my eleventh birthday. I wasn't surprised when I got it because my mom had prepared me for it a year earlier and let me practice wearing pads for when the time came (this is what I mean when I say she's my best friend and helps me a lot!). I had also read about it in Judy Blume's book *Are You There God? It's Me, Margaret* and the *American Girl* books.

I wasn't scared, but my period still posed a problem for me. I had an incredibly heavy flow and was scared of wearing tampons because I thought they hurt. Ask your mom, the school nurse or some other woman to help if you have questions.

Hair Removal, and Not the Hair on Your Head

Hair removal, or shaving of your armpits and legs, is another new venture for many girls in middle school. Your mom might tell you to wait, because once you start shaving you have to continue. But I think that if you have hair under your arms or on your legs, it is time to remove it. Throughout puberty you also grow hair in your pubic area and above your lips. It is normal. Don't panic. It is simply your hormones changing.

Generally, in our society at least, women remove only the hair under their armpits and on their legs. Of course, nobody says you have to remove the hair; besides, you may have sensory and other issues that prevent you from doing it. It is totally up to you.

Nevertheless, over the course of the middle school years, most girls give in to the hair-removal tradition, thinking it is embarrassing to be seen with hairy armpits and legs.

The pros of removing unwanted hair on your legs, armpits and upper lip are that you will fit in with most girls. If you don't shave, it is only a matter of time before other kids will notice and make fun of you behind your back.

Nobody talks about shaving or other ways of hair removal; in our society, it is just taken for granted after a certain age. It's like brushing your teeth or washing your hair – it is something that is expected. A warning – NEVER shave your eyebrows. They may NOT grow back.

1. **Shave.** Shaving is recommended for your legs, armpits and near your bikini line. Here are some tips about shaving. First, buy some shaving cream and a razor. I prefer to use the Gillette Venus® disposable razor because you don't get cut. I also use Skintimate® skin gel for sensitive skin because it is easy to spread.

Before you start shaving, it is a good idea to ask your mom or another experienced woman to show you how to do it properly. Don't apply too much pressure with the razor because you may cut yourself. If you do cut yourself, don't panic – the pain lasts only a few minutes, and you bleed, the tiniest little bit.

Once you start shaving, the hair grows back on your legs, armpits and bikini line within two to three days. So to continue the "hairless look," you need to shave on a regular basis. I think it is fun to shave, because I like seeing the hair come off.

2. **Electric razors.** These are also an option for shaving arms and legs. I didn't like electric razors because I didn't think my skin becomes smooth. The razor leaves my legs feeling stubbly.

3. **Waxing.** Waxing is another method used to re-move unwanted hair. It is especially used for your lip area if you have a lot of hair there (I'm talking like a mustache) and below your eyebrows (or if you are forming a unibrow). If you notice you are forming one eyebrow instead of two, that means the hair is growing along the bridge of your nose so that you have one thick line. As far as your upper lip goes, do not let this get out of control because kids will definitely notice a hairy lip and they will make fun of you.

When you have your eyebrows and lip area waxed, it stings a little bit the first time, but it isn't that bad. You can go to a salon to get waxed or you can buy a do-it-yourself kit at your local drugstore and have your mom or an older female relative or friend help you do it.

Waxing unwanted hair lasts longer than shaving – usually about four weeks, and the hair grows back lighter and is easier to remove each time. Each time it gets less painful.

4. **Smooth-Away**®. Another option for removing hair that is totally painless is a product called Smooth-Away. It is not incredibly accurate, but it is painless. You take the pad and rub it in circles on a hairy area and it gets rid of the unwanted hair. It doesn't take long, but it's hard to see where you did and didn't rub. This is a good product to try the first time if you're scared to shave or wax.

5. **Tweezers.** I recommend this for eyebrows only, and only after you've had them professionally shaped beforehand. When the person is shaping your eyebrows, you might feel a little tug when they remove the more stubborn hairs. It takes a little getting used to, but it gets easier and less bothersome each time you do it.

Finally, there are other ways of removing hair, including creams and going to a professional salon.

Chapter 6

While on the subject of hair removal, let's talk briefly about haircuts. In elementary school, it was cool to wear your hair in a ponytail every day. No one really noticed or cared what your hair looked like, but in middle school, people start noticing.

Before entering middle school, it is a good idea to get a good haircut. Look at hairstyles in magazines, on TV, etc. Pick a few out that you think would look good on you. Show or describe them to your hairstylist and ask for advice.

If you are not particularly interested in hairstyles and not good at working with your hair, be sure to get it styled in such a way that know you can take care of it. Looking good requires some time and effort. I still ask my mom to help me style my hair every day.

 I started shaving my legs and armpits at around the age of nine because I would swim a lot and my hair was abundant. My mom helped me do it the first couple of times, but after that I was on my own. By now, I'm quite good at it, to be honest. I used to be incredibly scared of waxing, but it doesn't hurt at all, and a year and a half after my love of tweezing, I got my eyebrows and lip waxed for homecoming (ninth grade).

I have found the best place to shave is in the bathtub. I suggest running warm water, and standing up.

Shave one leg at a time and then move up to your armpits. It is a good idea to ask your "superwoman" to change the blades on the disposable razors when they get dull. When they are dull, it is easier to cut yourself. Don't change them yourself because you can get cut.

Buying Bras

According to statistics, a lot of women wear the wrong bra size, which leads to a bunch of stuff like breasts sagging and backaches as women grow older. If you're in middle school, you should probably at least be wearing a training bra ("sports bra"). It's good to start early so that you get used to wearing a bra and it becomes second nature like wearing underpants.

If possible, shop somewhere that is known for accurately sizing girls and that carries smaller bra sizes. Most department stores have what you need. Don't freak out when the sales lady asks you to take your shirt off so she can measure you to determine the correct size bras to show you. Your parents probably told you not to let anyone, especially a stranger, see you naked, but if you go to a reputable store, it's okay. It's sort of like when you go the doctor.

Make sure you have a female adult with you when you go bra shopping. You don't need to have the prettiest bra, you need the best fitting one for your body and one that is affordable because you need more than one.

I started wearing a training bra before middle school. When I outgrew my training bras at the beginning of middle school, my mom took me to a department store where a woman took out a tape measure and measured my breasts. It was a bit freaky, but my mom had prepared me ahead of time for what was going to happen. Twice a year, my mom takes me to the store to get fitted for bras since my body continues to grow and change.

Staying in Touch with Style Trends

I know I have repeated myself about staying in touch with trends and how they work. Read magazines, observe what other kids are wearing and doing (only if you think it's right though – if you think the skirts are too short, then don't buy short skirts) and understand what people are talking about, whether it's the *American Idol* auditions or the new Jonas Brothers CD.

Having something to say about something that is popular helps a lot socially since you can fit in more easily when you have something to add to the conversation. A former friend of mine came up with a term to describe people: "sheeple." People are like sheep – they follow the herd and what a "leader" is doing. Knowing what that leader is doing is half the battle.

Fitting in is hard for everyone, especially us girls

with ASD. Like I said, you might not care about makeup and trends, but it will help you out socially more than you could imagine if you could understand what's going on. So let's look at some of these things.

Makeup

Applying and wearing makeup doesn't appeal to many girls on the spectrum. I don't like to wear it myself, but I think it is important to know how to put it on and here's why. First, almost everybody (even celebrities) looks better with makeup. Second, in the girl world, makeup gets you respected. When you wear makeup, other girls think you're cool and think you know what's going on socially, even if you don't really. Third, the other girls are not as likely to bully you because they see you as looking cool. Fourth, in case you're interested, many boys think you're pretty when you wear makeup.

When you go to the bathroom at school, you will see girls applying eyeliner, blush and lip gloss. Girls who don't wear makeup are almost looked upon as little kids. Most younger girls don't put makeup on properly, or they choose colors that clash with what they're wearing. The goal of makeup is to enhance what people look like naturally, not to look fake and mask-like.

A great idea is to have an older sister or your mom show you what to do with the brushes. Makeup is an art – it takes practice to get good at it. Another good idea is to go to the mall and ask a cosmetician at a makeup counter to choose your colors and make you up once. You don't have to buy everything at the counter, but just know your colors. You can often buy cheaper makeup at a drugstore that is just as good as department store brands.

I have to be honest – I ask my mom to help me apply makeup every morning. In sixth grade I started with lip gloss and blush. I worked my way up to eyeliner and eyeshadow, and finally mascara for special occasions.

A Teacher's Perspective

Target and Wal-Mart have makeup that is inexpensive and fun. Start slowly when you decide to start wearing makeup. As for your hair, it's important to get a haircut that fits your face. You can find popular haircuts, but if your hairstylist says it won't look good on your face, the majority of the time, it won't. A haircut that fits your face will look great, even if it's not the latest trend in hairstyles. And be sure you get a cut that you can easily take care of, even if you don't want to spend much time and effort on it.

Three Things You Need to Say No To: Sex, Drugs and Cheating

As part of your growing independence in middle school, you will have lots of decisions and choices to make. This goes way beyond clothes and friends to include serious issues that can affect the rest of your life – your health and well-being.

Sex and drugs. Two of the big ones are sex and drugs (drinking also counts under drugs because alcohol is a drug). You probably had a sex talk in elementary school and more in-depth in middle school, in addition to talking to your parents. So we won't repeat that here.

You have probably also had the drug talk by now. Drugs are serious. Doing drugs is a choice, and people usually do it because they feel depressed or because of peer pressure. Just because your friends are doing it, doesn't mean it's right. Remember the quote earlier, "What is right is not always popular, and what is popular is not always right." The drugs people get addicted to are illegal, and if caught with them, you could be arrested. No joke. They do arrest kids and put them in jail.

Advice From Other Girls on the Spectrum

Kids in middle school may make poor choices, such as smoking on school property. If you see this occur, wait until you are near a trusted adult in private and let them know about the situation.

Natasha

Cheating. Now for cheating. There are different kinds of cheating. When I talk about cheating and middle school, I'm referring to copying homework, plagiarizing textbooks, looking at your friends' work during a test and general academic cheating. Most schools have an honor code that is very specific with regard to three things: no lying, no stealing and no cheating. Nevertheless, all these things still happen at school, and the consequences can be bad. You need to learn how to say no to students who want to use you to copy your homework or use you because they know you are smart.

By letting a friend copy your homework, for example, you are cheating, too. You are an accomplice, because even though you're not copying yourself, you are letting someone copy your work. The way to get around copying (and still have friends) is to offer to help other kids with their homework, if you wish, instead of just giving them the answers. Your friends will not learn anything if they copy, so when it comes down to test time, they will not do well.

On the other hand, you would feel good if you were able to teach your friends, and they did well. Helping your friends makes you confident and gains the other kids' respect. They think you're a nice person for helping them and it will benefit them in the long run.

Plagiarizing from the Internet. Plagiarism is when you use someone else's idea or words and claim them as your own. So in a sense, it is a form of cheating. Plagiarism is becoming increasing common using the Internet. Do not copy directly off the Internet. Even if it doesn't seem that way, it's the same as using a textbook and copying it word for word. When writing a research paper, always cite your sources (give credit with a link or to an author) even if it is not required. Cover yourself – better safe than sorry. Also, don't use others' ideas word for word. Instead, paraphrase (rewrite/summarize), but still give credit to the original author for his or her research and thoughts on a topic. More than likely, your teacher will tell you how to do this in papers and on projects.

 My parents talked about things like this from an early age and my schools also did a bunch of things to teach us about the dangers of drugs, unprotected sex, etc. In fifth grade, my school did a program called GRADE (Gang Resistance and Drug Education) to show us the effects of drugs on the body and what gangs are and do. Your school probably has a similar program, even if called something else.

In sixth grade, my school didn't do anything in particular on these topics. In seventh grade, our school gave a presentation on the effects of sexually transmitted diseases, showed pictures of infected parts and explained the consequences. Not as much happened in eighth grade, because my school had an entire class about health, but we did have speakers on drugs who were ex-drug addicts. What I took way from all this is: Be careful; don't give in to peer pressure; stay healthy!

A Teacher's Perspective

If you are being pressured to have sex, do drugs or cheat, talk to a teacher you trust, the counselor or an adult in your life. Don't try to hide it or deal with it by yourself. Enlist the support of other people in your life that you can talk to. Situations like these are always difficult, and the more you can talk about it, the better off you'll be.

Chapter 7

STRESS AND ANXIETY

ntering middle/junior high school is a stressful time as there are a lot of unknowns and unfamiliar situations and people to get used to. When you don't know what to expect, that can make you nervous and anxious. This holds true for just about anybody, but for kids with ASD, who tend to have high anxiety in general, the stress can be especially challenging.

Most things that upset me in school revolve around other people and how they act. You need to realize that your friends are also nervous and anxious and also have bad days. This can affect the way they act toward you, so do not take everything personally. Everybody has bad moods and bad days – no one is perfectly happy all the time.

Everyone is sensitive to criticism. There will be times when someone will say something about you that is not nice. Sometimes we misunderstand what a person really means, so keep the comment inside your brain until you get home to talk to someone about it to see if you misread it or not. Then, if appropriate, decide what response to give.

Another thing that can cause extra anxiety is if you don't do well on a test. Find out what you did wrong, keep your feelings inside and ask for help. If you didn't do well, it just means you did not understand the material or were in a hurry and didn't think when you wrote down the answer. There is also the possibility that the teacher made a mistake grading your test.

Regardless, ask your teacher to look at the test and, if appropriate, explain the concepts to you. She may not be able to do it on the spot, so be patient and ask when is a good time to talk to her.

Everyone handles stress differently. Some kids plan ahead to help them deal with stress because it makes them feel organized and in control. If you are like that, one good thing is that you're reading this book, so it should help relieve some of the stress you may be feeling about unknowns.

To deal with stress, I "downloaded" when I got home from school. That is, I shut off my brain and took a half hour to myself to – either listening to music or playing video games. It is a good idea to do something you enjoy for about thirty minutes after school or before you start your homework. Another good way of coping with stress is to take a long, warm bubble bath. I usually do this with a good book. I could do this for so long that the water begins to get cold.

Do something that gets your mind off of things, even if it's playing with a stress ball or twirling your hair. Sometimes keeping your hands busy helps calm you down. I don't know why. When I get stressed or bored sometimes I twirl my hair or play with my earrings.

When you start to get anxious at school, try to stay calm. Then when you get home, you can let all your feelings out. Write them down in a diary, or talk to your parents or someone you can trust about your day. Do NOT break down, tantrum or cry during the school day. Never hit your desk, a wall, a student or a teacher when you get frustrated. When you're nervous in a class, spin or play with your pencil, twirl your hair or play with your jewelry. If my day is absolutely horrible and I am in class, I draw and work on a detailed picture to get my mind off of what I was upset about.

In elementary school teachers may have said to go to bed early the night before a test and eat a good breakfast the next morning. This and being wide awake helps you feel more energized and less stressed.

In elementary school you may also have learned some self-regulation skills. These things still apply in middle school. Keep using what's worked for you in the past, for starters at least. If something is really bothering you emotionally or socially, talk to a parent, trusted adult or the guidance counselor at your school.

Something to realize from middle school and beyond is that everyone makes mistakes, fails tests, doesn't get chosen for a team or is unsuccessful at a particular task. Everything is a learning experience. Remember that everyone is good at something. You need to find out what your "something" is. School can help you find out what your "something" is, whether it is math, geography, playing volleyball or being a superior violinist.

I never found academics stressful in middle school; it was the social aspects that posed challenges. On my desk at home, I had a stress ball to squeeze and keep my hands busy if I got bored or nervous (this has also helped me break my nail-biting habit since I used to do that when I was stressed). Also, I "download" and do something I enjoy after school to calm down after a long day. Take your dog for a walk, read a book, play a game, listen to music – don't just go straight to homework. Some may call this procrastination, but if it works for you to be recharged and calm when you start your homework, go for it.

For some students, holding their feelings inside is not a good idea. If something is really bothering you or you are extremely stressed out, it is best to ask to take a break, go to the bathroom, get a drink or ask to go talk to the counselor. It takes practice dealing with stressful situations, so don't worry if you still struggle with that. When you are calm and relaxed, try to brainstorm options that you can try when you are anxious and stressed out. Write them down on a card and slip it into your binder. When you start feeling stressed out, pull out your card and try one of the strategies listed.

Chapter 8

Hopes for the Future – High School and Beyond

The good news is that the transition to high school usually isn't nearly as drastic and traumatic as the transition from elementary to middle school. As the years go by, things for me have gotten a lot easier socially.

The first thing I realized about high school is that there is a lot more freedom than in middle school. There are lots of classes you can take, more clubs you can join and there are more people than in middle school, so the opportunities to make new friends are always there.

Different Is Cool

I know this is hard to believe when you're in middle school where everyone wants to fit in and be part of groups, but in high school people are a lot more accepting of who you are. Being an individual becomes the new trend. There are kids in my school from countries such as Latvia and they have tons of friends, there are people who are homosexual, people who are jocks, artists, computer nerds, and math geeks, and people are accepting of that's who their peers are. It's easier to make friends since there are many different types of kids and everyone is just more accepting of each other in general.

More Choices and More Annoying Things

In high school you are given opportunities to find yourself and start to discover what you want to do with your life. There are lots of clubs to join, sports teams, things to go to and people to meet, but there is also more homework and more competition because people are trying to do well because everything counts towards college. In high school you need to stay on track and not get distracted by simple things such as phone calls, noises, and even yourself sometimes.

A Teacher's Perspective

If high school seems scary to you, try some of the things that you did before beginning middle school. Walk through your schedule before school starts, find your locker and combination and try to find a teacher or counselor that you can talk to if you have problems. You'll find a lot more kids in high school, but you'll also find that there are more opportunities for you to find activities and classes that you'll like.

Conclusion

I hope this book has helped make you ready for middle school. And I hope you enjoyed the ride. As you have probably guessed by now, middle school was a bumpy road for me. I excelled academically, but socially not so much. I had a few friends, but for the most part I found it hard to relate to my peers. The one good thing is that I was never bullied or teased, mostly because I won the girls' respect because I was smart and I looked a certain way.

By the time you read this book, I will be a sophomore in high school. High school has been a very positive experience for me. I didn't have to switch schools, I have a few good friends and am accepted by my peers for who I am – a young woman with autism.

Towards the end of my freshman year, I had an opportunity in English class to tell my peers I am different. My first art show was coming up, and on the invitation, I openly came out as a person with autism. I never felt the need to tell people I had autism in middle school because everyone is so closed-minded and worried about fitting in that I didn't want to take the chance of being automatically rejected for being different. In middle school, different is "weird," but in high school, different is the new fitting-in.

Keep your hopes up, look good, act happy and be proud of who you are. There is nothing to be ashamed of or embarrassed about – most of us on the spectrum are gifted and talented in many different ways!

P.O. Box 23173
Shawnee Mission, Kansas 66283-0173
877-277-8254
www.aapcpublishing.net

CPSIA information can be obtained
at www.ICGtesting.com
Printed in the USA
LVOW05s1010211117
557076LV00004B/20/P